THE
SUSPENDED
SENTENCE

A Guide for Writers

THE
SUSPENDED
SENTENCE

A Guide for Writers

==

ROSCOE C. BORN

CHARLES SCRIBNER'S SONS
New York

For D. J.—of course

Library of Congress Cataloging-in-Publication Data

Born, Roscoe C.
The suspended sentence.

Includes index.
1. Journalism—Authorship.   2. English language—
Rhetoric.   I. Title.
PN4783.B67   1986   808'.06607   86-6673
ISBN 0-684-18672-1

Published simultaneously in Canada by
Collier Macmillan Canada, Inc.
Composition by Maryland Linotype, Baltimore, Maryland
Manufactured by Fairfield Graphics, Fairfield, Pennsylvania
Designed by Ruth Kolbert
First Edition

CONTENTS

CONTENTS

CONTENTS

CONTENTS

Preface

I was still shaking sand out of my clothes after a retirement fling in Florida when Bill Giles, then the editor of the *Detroit News,* was on the phone trying to lure me at least partway out of retirement. Would I, he asked, consider becoming a writing consultant to the *News?* I would not have to leave my woods in the exurbs of Washington, D.C., he assured me; he would send the newspaper and packets of copy to my home, and I could fly to Detroit every few weeks to talk to members of his staff about what I had found and how they could do better.

I had met Giles 25 years earlier, when we were on the staff of the *Wall Street Journal,* he in New York and I in the Washington bureau. Later, when Dow Jones conceived the *National Observer,* he (as the editor) and I were among four *Wall Street Journal* staffers who got the chance to bring the new national newspaper to life. One thing we wanted to do was make it a writer's paper, and I like to think it became known for that. The *Observer* died 16 years later, but something about our time together there, I guess, made Giles think I could help in Detroit. So I agreed to try.

As it turned out, Giles left Detroit a few months after I started, but his successor was another colleague from *Observer* days, Lionel Linder, who urged me to continue. It was he who saw that the periodic memos I was writing to his staff (as one part of the Detroit project) had a far wider use. Each of my little essays, he argued, dealt with a single writing problem, and the problems were universal; writers everywhere could read them and become better writers. In fact, other editors were asking for copies of the memos. So Linder suggested they should be collected into a book, and without even a show of modesty, I permitted myself to be convinced.

Here, then, are those memos, little changed from the way they were written and distributed to the editors and writers in Detroit. The chief difference is that in the originals, for obvious reasons, the examples of errant writing I cited were from the *Detroit News*. For this collection, I have substituted some examples found in many other publications, from Honolulu to Boston and south. Nobody has a monopoly on slipshod writing.

I thank Lionel Linder for his suggestion and the *Detroit News* for its interest in good writing and for letting me make public my close scrutiny of its columns, a process that has been going on for more than three years. I hope that Linder is right in believing that the campus journalist, the young professional, and maybe even an old pro might benefit from reading these essays. I further hope that *anyone* who writes— or is simply interested in writing—will enjoy them.

ROSCOE C. BORN *Brinklow, Md.*

=

INTRODUCTORY NOTES

=

Can good writing be taught, or must you have it in the genes? Eliminate the bad and leave the good to flourish.

Those writers and editors I see on my Detroit visits will find some familiar lines in this memo and in those that follow. For them these will serve as *aide-mémoire*. (It pleases me to presume that *some* of you, at least, will want to remember what was said.) And by reading these memos, those who have not attended our meetings may learn what the devil we do there, month after month.

What we do, primarily, is talk about good writing (and editing), but so far we have done it more by indirection. Although I do flash an occasional example of good writing, I confess I concentrate more on the shock value of bad examples—from the *Detroit News* and other papers.

I read the *News* regularly, scissors at the ready; when I find sinful doings, I clip out the noxious paragraph and paste it in a green notebook. At our Detroit meetings, I have read extensively from this collection.

Thus it might appear, at first glance, that I find the

News preponderantly bad. Not so. Viewing the whole newspaper, I find it superior to most dailies I have read. Although my green book fattens constantly, it's surprising how big a mound of newspapers I must burrow through to glean a few clips. It is these I delight in reading aloud, not because I am mean, but in the hope that to deride mischief is to diminish it, leaving the good to flourish.

That is also the basis for my general answer to the frequent question, Can you really teach somebody to be a good writer? This is almost always asked with a look and a tone that suggest that the asker wants the answer to be no. Believing himself to be a good writer, by way of his genes, he would like to be reassured that the club is open only to others with similar blue-blood talent.

If we are talking about brilliant writing, perhaps that is true. Years ago Jack Woodford sold a lot of how-to books on writing, based on his conviction that there were techniques that could be taught. But he also argued that you could never be truly great unless you had inherited intelligence, you had drama in your soul, and your glands—particularly your thyroid—functioned properly. Now that's really relying on the genes.

Similar arguments abound. Frederick L. Allen wrote a splendid little piece more than 60 years ago that divided people into two types: those with a heavy touch and those with a light touch. The heavies, he contended, made poor writers, stout fellows though they might be.

Allen classified George Washington as a heavy, Lincoln as a light. Gladstone had a heavy touch, Disraeli a light. The writing of the heavies, Allen wrote, "suggests the sort of oatmeal served at lunch counters, lumpy and made with insufficient salt. It is to be found at its best in nature books, railroad catalogs, and prepared speeches by high public officials."

Allen wouldn't say the heavies lacked a sense of humor. Many, in fact, have a "perfectly good standardized sense of humor," he wrote. "They laugh as hard as anybody else at a farce, and when an after-dinner story is told they shout mightily with the rest. [But] they regard humor as something embodied normally in jokes. . . . What they lack is the playful mind." And lacking a playful mind, they could never be great writers. In effect, you must be born a great writer.

Right now, though, we're talking about *good* writing, and if good writing cannot be taught, at least it can be learned by anybody with a sense of logic and reason who cares enough and has pride enough to be a good writer—and is willing to work hard enough, I hasten to add. If you discover that you cannot learn to be a good writer, perhaps we should fall back on that gene argument and suggest you go into tree surgery or the diplomatic service. *Some* basic talent, after all, is necessary.

I think you can learn to be a good writer in roughly the same way a newspaper can be improved: by striving to eliminate the negative. By first learning what is wrong and then how to avoid it, you are a better writer, just by the process of elimination.

That sounds easy, but it isn't. It demands a self-discipline that is constant and uncompromising. If you compromise just once and accept a sentence that isn't the very best way to say what you want to say, you are losing your virtue. I repeat: You must have enough pride to insist that *every* sentence is the best sentence you can write to say what must be said. If you write yourself into a muddle, don't try to salvage the sentence by bending it in another direction or tacking something onto the end. Throw it all out and start over. Every time.

Similarly, it is your own pride in your work that will stop you from using a word that may not mean precisely what you intend. If, in your writer's conscience, you hear the slightest whisper of doubt about that word, you will look it up; close enough will never do.

It is pride in your own work that will make you tend carefully to such seeming trivia as the comma, the semicolon, and (Lord, bless it!) the period, because to botch punctuation is to botch what otherwise might have been a bell ringer of a sentence.

Some writers contend that they have no time to bother with all these details. That long-delayed paper is finally due, a free-lance piece has been promised tomorrow, or the deadline for the next edition is 30 minutes away. But whether you use the half hour until deadline to turn out clear, concise prose depends on how well you have disciplined yourself in everything you have written before. What you *have* written is only preparation for what you are *going* to write. If you are constantly in training, you are ready for the quick draw and the bull's-eye shot. You cannot wait till High Noon to learn how to load your revolver.

But I perorate prematurely. An introductory note is not the place to hold forth about the passions of writing. That will come later, when I plan to turn positive and talk about things to do, not just things to avoid. For the moment, though, we'll accentuate the negative.

Stray Notes

All these are wrong:
From the *Richmond* (Va.) *Times-Dispatch:*

> A friend . . . convinced him to become an apprentice.

From the *Miami Herald:*

> A chemistry professor convinced him to get a degree in science.

From the *Philadelphia Inquirer:*

> . . . and then called Schmutz, who convinced him to surrender.

From the *Washington Times:*

> Different techniques were used in the four states in an effort to convince Democrats to change parties.

Persuade was the proper word in all four examples, not *convince*.

Although *persuade* can do double duty, it's easier to remember the distinction if you limit *persuade* to action. That is, you *persuade* somebody to do something, but you *convince* somebody of the wisdom (or folly) of something.

He convinced me that the stock market would rise would be correct. But: *He persuaded me to buy heavily in several stocks.*

Memory aid: *Convince* cannot be followed by an infinitive.

2

THE SUSPENDED SENTENCE

The biggest single step a writer (or editor) can take to improve readability: Don't block the flow of the sentence.

The title of this essayette may mislead you momentarily. It does not allude to some happy felon put back on the street by a permissive judge. It is, rather, my name for a writing practice that strangles all too many newspaper stories. I chose the name fully aware of the possibility for confusion—enjoying it, in fact, because I like the connotation that what I am about to denounce here should be regarded as downright criminal.

I would even venture that the biggest single step a writer could take to improve his style would be to stamp out the suspended sentence almost every time it is detected.

By my definition, to suspend a sentence means to start a sentence with the subject, then immediately halt its progress while the author shovels in miscellaneous (and sometimes extraneous) facts. Finally the author closes out his interstitial remarks and tacks the predicate onto the end of the whole messy business. By this time the reader has bogged down and turned to something else or has so lost the course of the sentence that he has to refer back to the subject to find out what is being said.

Here's an example:

> George A. Bridges, who was arraigned in
> city court yesterday on the charge of
> nonsupport of his wife and two minor
> children, whose case was continued in order
> that he could get $500 bail for his release,
> to comply with an order to pay $7 a week
> for his family's support, was released today
> on bail.

I selected that example from a collection of old front pages; this one happens to be from the *Evening Journal*, Wilmington, Delaware, December 20, 1913. The writer managed a 48-word suspension between subject and predicate.

It's easy to laugh at that and jeer at the quaint writing practices of the bad old days. But 70 years later the problem persists. Here's another example, a 45-word suspension, that I found in copy recently written by a *Detroit News* staff writer:

> The 33-year-old, 40-room mansion—with
> its formal rooms, parquet teakwood floors,
> recessed lighting, walk-in silver storage
> vaults, 20 electric refrigerators, 11 fireplaces
> and eight chimneys, flower rooms,
> bedrooms, guest and sitting rooms, servants
> quarters, third-floor theater, with a pool

> alongside a stone wall studded with
> gargoyle heads—was torn down in 1966.

It's enough to make one blaspheme. In fact, I *did* blaspheme when I read it. The person who wrote that knows better now, I think, and will never sin so heinously again. I confess that that sentence was in unedited copy and may never have seen print, so perhaps it's unfair to cite it as an example. All right, here's one that did appear in the *News:*

> Mark Moseley, who set a record last Sunday
> on the snow-slickened field at RFK Stadium
> in Washington when he kicked his 21st
> field goal without a miss to give the
> Washington Redskins a victory over the
> New York Giants, goes about his job
> straight away.

Well, say this for the writer: While he had the abdomen of that sentence cut open, he might have stuffed in the score, the distance Moseley kicked the thing, the time left to play, and the crowd reaction.

Similarly obstructed by a fact-filled suspension is this sentence, from the *Baltimore Sun:*

> Midshipman Campbell, a graduate of the
> Baltimore Polytechnic institute's "A"
> course who earned a combined Scholastic
> Aptitude Test score of 1,210 of a possible
> 1,600 and was team captain in three varsity

sports, said he learned that any question
has only five appropriate responses.

Here's one from the *Washington Post* that gets
suspended twice:

> The investigator, Claude H. Harris, who is
> heading the probe for the National
> Transportation Safety Board, said it is not
> yet known whether the medication, which
> is under study and had not been precisely
> identified last night, could have affected
> the driving ability of driver George B——,
> 68, or had a bearing on the crash.

In the *Chicago Tribune* we find this: a suspension
immediately followed by a parenthetical suspension:

> On that opening night, a fellow named
> Dennis DeYoung, the lead singer of the
> rock band Styx and a person whose
> attendance was highly coveted by the
> Limelight honchos ("We would love to send
> a limousine for Mr. DeYoung and his wife,"
> the Limelight folks gushed and gushed
> again even after hearing that the DeYoungs
> live a full 45 minutes away), arrived on
> foot, made his way around the waiting mob
> and, without mentioning his name, entered.

Care to try for three? The *New York Daily News*
did:

> Godard, once a dazzling New Wave
> wonder who has in recent years fallen from
> grace—most recently he has been
> denounced by the Pope himself for this
> year's "Hail Mary," a rather less than pious
> portrait of the Virgin—remains Godard.

See how disturbing a suspension can be? You follow that trail carefully to the end and suddenly you hit this bump: *remains Godard*. It is meaningless, unless you retrace your steps; then you discover that the basic sentence is *Godard remains Godard*.

The next suspension, from the *Detroit News*, presents a slightly different problem:

> The other two men—William H——, 50,
> owner of Morgan Aviation, a Mojave,
> Calif., aircraft service firm; and Steven
> A——, 34, of San Diego—were arrested
> and charged earlier.

That's only a 20-word suspension, but it is complicated by all the punctuation it required: seven commas, one period, and one semicolon. That's just too many hurdles blocking the direct flow of the sentence and straining the reader's attention span.

Sometimes it's not just the length of the suspension that befuddles or annoys the reader. Repeated interruptions—even short ones like this—can do the same thing, as these opening sentences from three consecutive paragraphs illustrate:

> The premier, who used his parliament
> forum to announce the mass release of
> dissidents and other conciliatory moves,
> said . . .
>   Gen. Jaruzelski, wearing his summer
> khaki uniform, added . . .
>   The general, who also heads the
> Communist Party, had . . .

Damn the general's summer khakis! Let's get on with it. There's nothing indecent about a sentence that runs directly from subject to predicate. Why cover its middle with a fig leaf?

To make a story flow, the sentences must flow. They provide the action that moves the story along, taking the reader with it. Sentences can't do that job if they're choked off midcourse time after time. That is true of any kind of writing.

Take a look at some of our time-tested fiction if you believe that the kind of straight-arrow sentence I am advocating is mere "Run, Spot, Run" writing. Check out your favorites. You'll search most of their pages in vain for sentences that have been suspended, forcing the reader to drift through stagnant pools of facts before picking up the current of the sentence again.

But, some may protest, I *want* to include a lot of facts. Well, of course. But a sentence that sets out to narrate Fact A is not the place to jam in Facts B, C, and D unless you can do it unnoticed, without blocking the flow. In general, use one sentence to convey one idea, and we'll all be the better for it.

The suspended sentence is not a way to *write* facts. It is a way of printing them out, like a computer-generated chart or graph, with no regard to the lilt or rhythm that marks good prose.

Stray Notes

From the *New York Daily News:*

> Sara and Ikhil K—— of Forest Hills died
> after eating kapchonka laced with the
> deadly botulin toxin.

Now I know that the most notorious of recent poison epidemics produced thousands of news stories about a painkiller that had been *laced* with poison. All right, some nut had indeed laced the medicine with poison—that is, he had *added a dash* of poison to it. But that doesn't mean that, for evermore, everything that is poisonous has been *laced*. Nobody added a dash of botulin to the kapchonka; it just grew there. This is another example of the danger in grabbing a popular word or phrase and sticking it into a story without bothering to find out what it means.

HOW
TO
SHOOT
A SENTENCE

The sentence as a rifle shot, not a buckshot load of facts sprayed in the general direction of the target.

Suspending a sentence is only one way to kill its effectiveness, to block its direct flow and leave the reader stranded. Here's another way that's closely related and just as obstructive.

Hold on, some of you may say; can't we stop fooling around with sentences and talk about good writing? And I say that until we can consistently write sentences that convey our meaning instantly and unmistakably, good writing is impossible—even we have raw talent oozing from every pore.

For reinforcement I call up the late Wilson Follett, who had this to say in his *Modern American Usage:*

> This principle comes close to summing up
> the secret of good writing: No one should
> ever be called upon to read a sentence twice
> because of the way it is constructed. We
> may like to read a sentence twice or 20
> times because its contents are profound,
> subtle, suggestive, and challenging. . . . But
> the writer who keeps making us retrace
> because of the way his sentences are put

> together is foisting on his reader his own
> proper work. To do so is laziness; and
> whatever it may be deemed elsewhere,
> laziness in a writer is the gravest sin.

Let me make it clear that I am not simply advocating short sentences; I dislike the staccato effect that results from an unbroken string of short sentences. I would prefer short sentences, though, to the problem we face. Our problem is the convoluted sentence, the sentence that meanders through a maze of clauses so that the writer himself gets lost—and *he* certainly has a better crack at it than the reader gets. I'm talking about not only clauses but stray phrases and handfuls of facts that make the sentence long and complex.

This is the view of Herbert Read in his book *English Prose Style:* "Many such sentences are often in the nature of an agglomeration of inconsistent and unrelated clauses, and should really be split up into several sentences." Readers get confused, he says, "because we so often come to a point [that] completes the sense of a possible sentence within the sentence."

In short, a sentence that tries to convey too many ideas runs a high risk. Here's an example from the *Detroit News:*

> There are practice greens to chip to and
> bunkers to play out of, and it is no wonder
> private-club members are more adept at
> those shots than public-course players—
> private-club players have a pleasant place

> to practice, and they can accomplish
> something.

I'm not just complaining about the 45-word length of that sentence; some sentences that long or longer can be read in a breeze. This one is sloppy. The length of this sentence should have sounded an alarm to the writer (and to his editor) that something might be wrong. My own rule of thumb is that if I have written three lines without hitting a period, I had better reexamine my sentence. After review, I may decide that the sentence is sound and let it proceed. But I am forced to audit my work on the spot if I have filled three typewritten lines.

Another clue here should have been the number of *and*s. That sentence from the *News* contains three, and two of them sent the sentence off in new, unexpected directions. Again, I'm not saying there's a fixed number of *and*s permitted in a sentence. I am saying that the writer and editor should have pricked up their ears at the sound of a third *and* (if not at the second) and reviewed the sentence then and there. Had they done so, they surely would have recast it along these lines:

> Private-club players have a pleasant place
> to practice and they can accomplish
> something. They have practice greens to
> chip to and bunkers to play out of. It is no
> wonder they are more adept at those shots
> than public-course players.

The next example is from raw copy, written for the *Detroit News* and reproduced here exactly as it was written:

> But Norton Zinder, professor of Microbial Genetics at Rockefeller University, though agreeing fraud does exists in science, disagreed that the three checking mechanisms were created to detect fraud, that it is individual psychopathology rather than the nature of scientific pursuit that creates fraud and that fraud in science is not prevalence.

Now let's see if we can sort this out. It's clear that Zinder agreed that fraud does exist in science, but he

(1) "disagreed that the three checking mechanisms were created to detect fraud."

I take that to mean that Zinder says the three mechanisms were *not* created to detect fraud. But when that story appeared in the *News*, it included this sentence: *Norton Zinder, a professor at Rockefeller University, said the checks were created to detect fraud*—just the opposite of what I took the writer's original sentence to mean. But I presume the editor discussed it with the writer and ascertained his meaning—a privilege denied to the reader.

(2) disagreed "that it is individual psychopathology rather than the nature of scientific pursuit that creates fraud."

I interpret that to mean Zinder believes the fraud *is*

created by the nature of scientific pursuit. The edited version of this story did not attempt an interpretation, choosing to eliminate that thought, but my guess is that the writer again meant the opposite of what he wrote.

(3) disagreed "that fraud in science is not prevalence."

Prevalent, of course, the writer meant. But he also meant, I think (and the editor decided), that Zinder denied that fraud is prevalent in science—again, the opposite of what he wrote.

But the point is, Why should a reader have to stop and interpret what a sentence means, even if it's possible, upon close examination, to figure it out correctly? I would venture that *no* reader would have even tried to sort out the meanings of the various thoughts the writer stuffed into that 51-word sentence. (The writer's internal alarm system should have sounded about halfway through the sentence, warning him of impending peril.)

This is the lead paragraph of a page 1-A story:

> Preliminary examination of control tower tapes and scattered wreckage has given federal safety investigators no immediate clues to the cause of the crash which killed three veteran airline pilots when their four-jet cargo plane plunged into a muddy field shortly after takeoff yesterday from Detroit Metropolitan Airport.

That's just jamming too much into a single sentence, especially a lead. Surely *some* of that information could have been deferred for another sentence or sprinkled in harmlessly as the story proceeded. (Or did it proceed? After a lead like that, was there anything more to say?)

I grant that that sentence, at least, heads in a single direction. Some readers probably can plow through it in one attempt, but others might stumble over all those facts and have to retrace. (Few will bother; once lost, they give up.)

I would have given up on this one, from the *New York Times:*

> Officer P——'s grand jury testimony, given in May and November of 1984, was the first account of what occurred while Officers K——, P—— and Henry B—— had Mr. S—— in a van traveling between First Avenue and 14th Street, where he had been arrested for writing graffiti at a subway station, and the transit police district command at Union Square West.

Now take a breath and read this sentence, also from the *New York Times:*

> The developments in the reconstruction project come after revelations that an extensive effort by the Goode Administration to repair damages at 82

houses nearby the destroyed homes has been plaqued [sic] by shoddy workmanship, double-billing by contractors, inadequate management controls and ongoing disputes over how much damage was caused by the May 13 siege in which a police bomb ignited a blaze that killed 11 people and became the worst residential fire in Philadelphia history.

Then try this one from the *Los Angeles Times:*

The brief, filed on behalf of 68 House members and 13 senators led by California Rep. Don Edwards (D-San Jose) and Sen. Bob Packwood (R-Ore.), said that overturning the Roe decision would "cast into grave doubt" a variety of rulings dating from 1923 that invoked parental and family autonomy and provided the legal foundation for Roe vs. Wade because, if the high court were willing to reverse the Roe decision it might be willing to reverse the others.

I sense that you're groggy by now, but I can't resist one more example, this one from the *Philadelphia Inquirer:*

Fahrenkopf said the program had spawned numerous benefits . . .

(I set aside the question of whether something beneficial can be *spawned*. I doubt it, but let it pass.)

> ... by generating campaign-year
> enthusiasm among party workers in a
> non-campaign year, improved voter lists,
> stronger party organizations in four states
> with hotly contested Senate races next year
> and, sooner or later, 100,000 new
> Republicans.

Perhaps I'm just inattentive, but I had to retrace my way through that sentence. I would prefer something like this:

> Fahrenkopf said the program improved
> voter lists, strengthened party organizations
> in four states that expect close Senate races
> next year, and created—sooner or later—
> 100,000 new Republicans. It also produced
> intangible benefits by generating
> campaign-year enthusiasm among party
> workers in a noncampaign year.

To sum up, I repeat Follett's maxim: No one should ever have to read a sentence twice. That, he says, "comes close to summing up the secret of good writing."

One way to follow his advice is to think of a sentence as a rifle shot—one missile, precisely aimed—rather than a scattershot load sprayed in the general direction of the target. If you can make one thought, or one nugget of information, instantly clear in a single sentence, that's enough. Your sentence runs into trouble when you try to pack two or four or six thoughts into it and shoot them all at the reader at once. You'll miss.

Stray Notes

═══

I could work up a full head of steam about this, but the problem requires little explanation, so perhaps these notes will do.

From the *Houston Chronicle:*

> R—— has admitted participating earlier this year in a series of thrill bombings with targets ranging from a telephone booth to a portable toilet.

From the *Los Angeles Times:*

> Three people were jailed on a variety of charges, ranging from prostitution to resisting arrest and reckless driving.

From the (Portland) *Oregonian:*

> She plans to discuss her opinions and activities, ranging from collecting antiques

to working with other Senate wives to promote use of warning labels on rock 'n' roll records.

The *St. Louis Post-Dispatch:*

. . . ranging from a lack of preparation for fires to poor control over medications.

Here, the *Honolulu Star-Bulletin and Advertiser* does not use *range*, but it purports to state one anyway, with the same results:

That conference will touch on everything from health care cost containment through the impact of news media on political institutions.

The *Wall Street Journal* says a Cincinnati company makes *products ranging from roofing to computer tape.*

And to complete this roundup, the *Washington Post* writes of *problems ranging from alcoholism to inability to manage funds.*

What kinds of ranges are these? From prostitution to reckless driving? What's in between? What's in a range between a telephone booth and a portable toilet? Between roofing and computer tape?

Range means "everything between this limit and that

limit," and the reader must be able to visualize what's between them. Everything from one to ten or from A to L. Everything between First Street and Fourth Street. Ranging from Maine to Florida. The examples previously quoted speak of no true ranges at all.

MISPLACED
PARTS

Sentence parts, that is. Detecting a third major sentence fault that will cool a reader's interest.

For the sake of variety, I'll open this time with an example that's *not* from a newspaper:

> That was supposed to help the Allies
> because in practice most of the arms sales
> would be to Britain and France, both at
> that time better able financially to buy them
> and to ship them across the Atlantic than
> Nazi Germany.

My safety requires that I not identify the source of that sentence, except to say that it's from the autobiography of a noted writer I have often praised. Here, however, he has let his guard down and has illustrated what I deem to be a third major sentence fault: the misplaced part.

Does this sentence violate Follett's maxim and force the reader to read it twice? Well, perhaps not, but it's close. It did slow me down, certainly, all because of a misplaced part. If you haven't recognized the offending part already, it is the phrase *than Nazi Germany*, hanging there at the end.

Maybe I'm too much of a literalist, but what that sentence says to me, at first read, is that it costs less to ship arms across the Atlantic than across Nazi Germany. Did I seriously believe that the writer meant that? Not for more than a millisecond, perhaps, but the thought flickered through my mind and diverted my attention. Had it not, I would have read right through, and the sentence would never have become a matter of remark.

Often the writer or editor can simply move the misplaced part to its proper place and correct a problem sentence. That can be done here by making it read: *better able financially than Nazi Germany to buy them and to ship them across the Atlantic.* But even though the meaning is right, the sentence is still awkward. Better, in my view, to recast the whole thing (and tighten it a bit) along these lines:

> That was supposed to help the Allies. At
> that time, Britain and France had the means
> to buy the arms and ship them across the
> Atlantic; Nazi Germany could ill afford to.

That's eight words shorter than the original, contains all the original thoughts, and does not force the reader to stop and parse. (The parse that refreshes? I wouldn't touch the line.)

Here's one from the *Honolulu Star-Bulletin and Advertiser:*

> The penalties are already allowed under
> law and are being assessed against
> international travelers who try to smuggle
> prohibited products into the United States
> *and airline employes.*

By misplacing a part, the writer has made the sentence say something he didn't mean it to say. What he meant was: *assessed against airline employes and international travelers who try to smuggle prohibited products into the United States.*

Sometimes a misplaced part can do funny things to a sentence, as in this example from a *Detroit News* story about a drug raid:

> Jessica W——, 28, and Abernathy A——,
> 26, both of Detroit, were charged with
> delivery of cocaine *after the raid.*

Why would they deliver the stuff there after the raid? Of course, that's not what the writer meant. He meant: *after the raid, Jessica and Abernathy were charged with delivery of cocaine.* The time element was misplaced.

Here's an example from the *Miami Herald:*

> In the last 10 days, he and a handful of
> others have begun a letter-writing campaign
> to federal fishery management councils
> *with jurisdiction over kingfish* who will
> decide on the ban.

My twisted mind makes that read that the kingfish will decide on the ban. Mending this one is not so simple as moving a misplaced part to its proper place in the sentence. The solution here is to drop *with jurisdiction over kingfish*; the whole story is about kingfish and whether catching them will be banned, so this phrase isn't needed. Without it, the last part of the sentence would read: *to federal fishery management councils, which will decide on the ban.*

I found this one in *Fortune* magazine (written by a friend, who normally avoids such pitfalls):

> Hewlett-Packard has just introduced a
> $4,995 personal computer *for engineers*
> with a nine-inch electro-luminescent screen.

Talk about your market niche!

The misplaced part, of course, is *for engineers.* The sentence should read:

> For engineers, Hewlett-Packard has just
> introduced a $4,995 personal computer with
> a nine-inch electro-luminescent screen.

From the *Los Angeles Times:*

> In 1935 he joined the embryonic Basie
> group and remained with what many
> consider the greatest jazz organization of
> all time *until 1948.*

Because of the misplaced part, I take that to mean that after 1948 the Basie group was no longer considered the best of all time.

From the *Boston Globe:*

> As lead singer Paul Redman pranced on the stage, a woman, perhaps 70, smiled and watched, her hair drawn back in a tight bun and *dressed in a widow's black.*

Back to the *Detroit News:*

> Feikens is to make a final decision on how the contractors, Vista and Michigan Disposal Inc., can continue to haul Detroit sludge *in a meeting next Monday with their lawyers.*

I'll skip that meeting, if you don't mind. This one is similar:

> The Pistons' general manager wants a big guy who can bang the boards *in Tuesday's National Basketball Association draft.*

If it isn't the nose, it's the ears that suffer. Now this next one really did confuse me, and not just momentarily:

> Southfield police released 248 pages of material on Jewish and neo-Nazi groups they accumulated *while keeping track of political protests to the American Civil Liberties Union.*

Honestly, I thought at first that the police were keeping track of protests made to the ACLU. Several sentences later, finding myself in a daze, I traced back to see where I had gone astray. I found then that the police had released the files *to* the ACLU, not that the protests were to the ACLU. With the parts re-arranged to make that meaning clear, the sentence would read:

> Southfield police released to the American Civil Liberties Union 248 pages of material they had accumulated on Jewish and neo-Nazi groups while keeping track of political protests.

And finally, a real blunder:

> From his Santa Barbara ranch yesterday, Mr. Reagan quickly reacted to allegations of wrongdoing and possibly criminal conduct at the EPA *by a Michigan congressman.*

No matter what the sentence seems to say, I feel sure it was not a Michigan congressman who was accused of wrongdoing and possibly criminal conduct. It was the EPA. Field-stripped and reassembled, the sentence reads:

> From his Santa Barbara ranch yesterday, Mr. Reagan quickly reacted to a Michigan congressman's allegations of wrongdoing and possibly criminal conduct at the EPA.

If we are agreed that the misplaced part is a problem, what can we do to prevent it? I'm afraid I have no simple trick to suggest. You just have to develop an ear for the sour note that throws the whole sentence off key. That comes, over time, by exercising a self-discipline that, as I said earlier, is constant and uncompromising. You must insist that *every* sentence is the clearest you can write to say what must be said. If you feel you are losing control of a sentence, that you have left out some element that is vital, don't try to jam the missing element in at some inappropriate point or tack it onto the end. Throw it all out and start over. Every time. If you have any doubt about a sentence just completed, read it over and let it resonate in your ears. And if it doesn't ring true, rewrite it on the spot. If you work at this, eventually you sharpen your early-warning system so that the alarm rings automatically whenever a sentence goes awry.

Stray Notes

Consider this, from *Northwest Orient* magazine:

> One of Philip Johnson's only home
> appliances is a floor lamp that he . . .

One of the only? This is pure nonsense—and *Northwest Orient* is not one of the only publications to make that mistake.

Onliness is the condition of being alone, being one of a kind, unique. If a person says, *I am an only child*, the meaning is clear. What if he said, *I am one of the only children*? Utter confusion.

Northwest Orient should have written, *one of Philip Johnson's few home appliances*—if that is really what the sentence meant. One can only surmise.

UP
FROM
RHETORIC
ZERO

A nongrammarian's handy trick for solving the most frequent error: whom *or* who, whomever *or* whoever?

It was in the seventh grade that my proud teacher proclaimed me a genius at grammar. Chalk in hand, I could cover a blackboard with sentence diagrams in seconds. With a single shot I could bag a gerund in full flight. *Subjunctive mood* rolled as easily off my tongue as *nominative case.*

In the next six years I lost it all. As a university freshman, I was bounced out of Rhetoric I and into Rhetoric Zero, a no-credit class where I was to be confined until I could demonstrate a sufficient grasp of the rules and principles of grammar to rejoin the human race.

I stayed long enough to write one essay. The wise woman who taught this remedial course praised the essay, denounced the pedantry that had sent me there, and dispatched me back to Rhetoric I with a note guaranteeing safe passage. It is enough, she said, to be able to use the language correctly; it does not matter that you cannot recite the rules and principles of grammar. They are like training wheels, to be discarded when they have done their job.

I admit all of this to calm any fears you may have that I am about to deliver an academic dissertation on the laws of grammar. A refugee from Rhetoric Zero would never do that. What I am going to do, though, is point out some errors that have crept into contemporary writing and offer some simple preventives.

Consider this from the *Detroit News:*

> Now he faces the prospect of defeat
> because of the President, who many
> Democrats blame for Michigan's continued
> economic distress.

The error, I hope, leaped immediately to your eye. *Who* should have been *whom.* Unfortunately, my research discloses that *who/whom* confusion is one of the most common errors appearing in the American press.

Here's an example from the *St. Louis Post-Dispatch:*

> He becomes more and more confused by
> the goings-on, not knowing who he has
> killed.

Should it be *who* he has killed or *whom?* You need not be an accomplished grammarian to figure it out, if you apply a simple test to *who/whom* choices. Even though I think I know, I apply this test whenever I encounter a choice, just to make sure I have it right.

Here is all the grammatical knowledge you need to master this test: *Who* is used when the word wanted is the subject of a sentence or clause. So, in this sense, *who* belongs with the other pronouns easily recognized as subjects: *I, we, he, she,* and *they.* But *whom* is the correct word when it serves as the object, so it belongs with other objective pronouns: *me, us, him, her,* and *them.*

Now, when you are uncertain whether to use *who* or *whom,* first determine the clause the word appears in. In the first example above, the clause is *who many Democrats blame.* Next, mentally rearrange the order of the words in the clause, making it read *many Democrats blame who.* If the subjective *who* is correct, you should be able to substitute another subjective pronoun (in this example, *he*) for *who* and have it read correctly. What you have is *many Democrats blame he.* You see immediately that this is wrong, that it should read *many Democrats blame him.* You know *him* is a pronoun used as an object, so you want the objective *whom,* that is, *whom many Democrats blame.*

It only sounds complicated. With practice, you can put a *who/whom* choice to this test in an instant. Try it on the second example above: *who he has killed.* Mentally change the order of the words to *he has killed who.* If it isn't already apparent that *whom* is the word you want, try the pronoun substitution. Clearly, you wouldn't say *he has killed he*. You would say *he has killed him*, using the objective pronoun. So you want the objective *whom*.

Another example, from the *Philadelphia Inquirer:*

> John I—, 40, of Berlin, N.J., was arrested
> yesterday and charged with murder in the
> death of a 3-month-old boy who police
> said the man had beaten.

The relevant clause is *who police said the man had beaten*. Change the order to *police said the man had beaten who*. If *who* is correct, if a subject is what is wanted, you should be able to substitute *he*—another subjective pronoun—and make it read properly. But what you get is *police say the man had beaten he*. Obviously, it should be *him*, the object, and so it should be *whom*, the object.

Here are some tricky examples from the *Detroit News:*

> Although it had been assumed all along
> that Hipple would start . . . Clark avoided
> until yesterday making an official
> announcement on *whom his starter is*.

> Either you sit there and look at the passing
> scenery or engage in a light conversation
> with *whomever happens to be sitting
> nearby*.

It may seem, at first glance, that *whom* is the object of the preposition *on* in the first example and *whomever* the object of the preposition *with* in the second. So if they're the objects of prepositions, these writers may have reasoned, they should be objective: *whom* and *whomever*. Not so. The object of the preposition is actually the entire clause, in italics in each example above. What counts is how the word is used *in its own clause*.

So, as before, determine the clause and mentally change the order of the words in it. In the first example look at *whom is his starter* and substitute the objective pronoun *him* for *whom* to test whether you really want an object. Clearly, *him is his starter* is wrong. You want the subjective *he* and therefore the subjective *who* in the original clause.

In the second example, the clause is *whomever happens to be sitting nearby*. The writer here chose the objective form. Substitute the objective pronoun *him* and you have *him happens to be sitting nearby*. Wrong. It should read *he happens to be sitting*, so you need *whoever*, the subject, not *whomever*, the object.

From the *New York Daily News:*

> At each performance, the audience is asked
> to vote on whom they think the murderer
> is.

Mentally rearranged, the key clause is *they think whom is the murderer*. The writer used the objective *whom*, so substitute the appropriate objective pronoun, *him*. What you now have is *they think him is the murderer*. Even an illiterate knows that is wrong. The proper substitute is *he*, the subjective, so the writer wanted the subjective *who*.

Try the test on this, from the *Washington Post:*

> Edith N—— was charged Wednesday in
> the death of her son, David N——, whom
> police said was smothered Aug. 23 to keep
> him from crying.

I won't insult your intelligence or bore you numb by going through yet another step-by-step breakdown. Apply the test and you can readily see that the writer should have used *who*.

And this, from the *San Francisco Examiner:*

> Back to Ernestine, who I asked about the
> other important factor in any decision to
> buy a house.

Whom, of course.

(Part of this confusion may result from daydreaming in grammar school. The student who didn't listen when teacher explained *who/whom* and *I/me* is aware today that some people seem to use *whom* and *I* a lot. So, he catches himself when he is about to say *between you and me* and substitutes *I*—and is wrong, of course. If he finds himself about to say *who* in what he thinks is an unusual place in a sentence, he changes it to *whom*, without knowing why, and with a 50-50 chance of getting it wrong.)

I swear, this test is much harder to describe than it is to do. It is so easy to do that the *who/whom* error could be eradicated with little trouble.

What it comes down to is whether you care. One editor asked me recently if I thought it really mattered to the average reader whether we use correct grammar. I inferred that he meant the average reader wouldn't know the difference, so why bother?

Perhaps the "average reader," whoever that is, doesn't know. But if he doesn't, he certainly isn't going to call up or write a letter to complain that you *don't* use *incorrect* grammar. On the other hand, the literate reader will surely know the difference and think less of your publication if you are incorrect. He is likely to conclude that your newspaper doesn't know right from wrong, good from bad, and dismiss you as incompetent writers and editors. Your reputation will suffer, as an institution and as individual writers and editors.

Stray Notes

From the *Detroit News:*

> Just then James Bond twiddled his small toe
> and activated a gyro-message transmitter
> with a prearranged code.

In my view, unless both parties have agreed on a code, it's not a code. If it's a code, it necessarily was arranged or it wouldn't work. So *arranged code* would be redundant—and this one is *prearranged* yet! (I once knew a writer who insisted on writing *pre-planned.* I could never discover how that differed from just plain *planned.* I couldn't seem to get the point across to him, although I tried hard right up to the day he prepacked all the stuff from his desk and departed.)

RHETORIC ZERO (CONT.)

=

The No. 2 error: singular nouns with plural verbs, and vice versa. How easily we deceive ourselves!

Now that the words have cooled, I look back over the last memo and see that I opened with a banquet-hall introduction but then served up a solitary kebab. After that grand discourse about Rhetoric Zero, you might have expected more than a simple drill about *who/whom.*

Since the introduction was elaborate enough to cover several points of grammar, I now elect to spend the unused portion of it on another grammatical problem that, the evidence suggests, needs some attention.

The problem is number disagreement between subject and verb. But first, some of the evidence, from the *Detroit News.*

> In fact, only one of the 148 members of the incoming Legislature are older than Sullivan. He's Rep. John Bennett.

Most of you will recognize the problem at once. The subject of the sentence is *one*—a singular subject, without question. Yet the writer used the plural verb *are*. Discard the intervening words and you get *only one are*. The writer confused himself (and his editor) by the intervening words containing the plural *members*, which is *not* the subject.

Of course, everybody knows the correct verb was *is*. If this were an isolated error, it would hardly be worth mentioning. But number disagreements keep getting into print.

From the *Washington Post:*

> The Fairfax school system, like many other
> area schools, have no set formula.

Same problem. The intervening plural noun, *schools*, prompted the writer to use a plural verb, when the real subject, *the Fairfax school system*, is singular.

The reverse of this problem is illustrated by this, from *Investor's Daily:*

> ... but no requests for any specific action
> was made, a spokesman said.

Here an intervening singular, *any specific action*, threw the writer off. *Action* is not the subject; *requests* is the subject, and that is plural—*no requests ... were made*.

To quote Fowler: "Some writers are as easily drawn

off the scent as young hounds. They start with a singular subject; before they reach the verb, a plural noun
attached to an *of* or the like happens to cross, and off
they go in the plural; or vice versa. This is a matter
of carelessness or inexperience."

Once in a while, though, even a veteran writer can
go astray, hearing the sound of plural as the sentence
progresses and unwittingly setting down a plural verb.
That's when the writer, instead of damning all editors,
wishes he had one who could save him from embarrass-
ment, as the editors in the above examples failed to do.

Another kind of number disagreement, also from the
Detroit News:

> Miss LaRose said the park and a lot of
> nearby housing was built in the 19th
> century.

The writer had a compound subject—*the park and
a lot of nearby housing*—and needed the plural verb
were. I suspect he was thrown off because the noun
next to the verb was *housing*, a collective noun that,
standing alone, would indeed require *was*. But that
doesn't matter here. The subject was compound—two
nouns joined by *and*—and a compound subject needs
a plural verb.

Fowler again: "The compound subject is necessarily
plural, whether its components are both plural, or
different numbers, or both singular."

But be careful here. What may *look* like a compound subject may not be, as illustrated by this mistake from the *Washington Post:*

> A Montgomery County Humane Society
> spokesman said that heat exposure and
> dehydration were probably strong factors
> in the boa's death, adding that only extreme
> temperature or old age generally cause
> death to such an animal.

The writer must have mistaken *extreme temperature* and *old age* as two subjects joined into a compound, which would have been true if they had been joined by *and.* The plural *cause* then would have been correct. But they were joined by *or,* so each stands alone as a singular subject, sharing in turn a singular verb: *extreme temperature causes,* or *old age causes.*

These next examples, from the *Detroit News,* present a similar problem:

> Neither H—— nor W—— were available
> for comment.

> Neither W—— nor the resident, D——,
> were hurt in the attack.

> Neither of the first two albums were
> received well.

All of these writers appear to have believed they had compound subjects. Not so. As Fowler explains: "*Neither . . . nor* does not combine two singular subjects into a plural. . . ." In *neither/nor* (and *either/ or*), we have two subjects considered separately. So if both subjects are singular, as they are in these examples, the singular verb is correct: *Neither H—— nor W—— was available; neither W—— nor the resident . . . was hurt*. And the third example above actually means *neither one of the first two albums*, so the verb should be *was*.

Each often presents a similar problem, as in this example, from the *Denver Post:*

> . . . and the mother and daughter have
> learned how to communicate about the
> stress each are under.

Each is under, of course.

That's simple enough. So is the choice easy when both subjects are plural; they would require a plural verb. Example: *Neither the Redskins nor the Raiders were able to score in the first quarter.*

We run into trouble, though, when one of the *neither/nor* subjects is singular, one plural. Example: *Neither the President nor members of his Cabinet were (was?) aware of the crisis.*

What should the verb be?

I can pull two grammar books from the shelf that agree on a clear-cut answer. The verb should agree with the subject nearer to it, these books say. In the above example, the plural *members* is closer to the verb, so the verb should also be plural: *were* is correct.

Suppose the sentence had read *Neither the members of the Cabinet nor the President was (were?) aware of the crisis.* Here the subject nearer the verb is *President*, which is singular, so the rule requires that the verb be singular: *the President was.*

But I can also pull down Follett and find:

> Some grammarians encourage writers to make the verb agree in number with the nearest subject; but the clash will be felt by thoughtful readers. [Such a sentence would be] defensible, but a workmanlike writer may put pride in not writing sentences that need defending.

And Fowler, while acknowledging that the grammar books may be technically correct, is clearly annoyed by the sound of the rule in practice. Both Fowler and Follett prefer to evade the choice and reshape the sentence.

So where does that leave us with *neither/nor* when one is plural, one singular? Although my ear is not so affronted as Fowler's and Follett's by the sound of the correct usage, I would agree with them and take the coward's way out. "The wise man," Fowler counsels, "in writing, evades these problems by rejecting all the alternatives—any of which may set up friction between him and his reader—and putting the thing in some other shape."

Another problem with subject-verb agreement is illustrated by this, from the *Houston Chronicle:*

> Mitzi is one of the few *people who hears from her.*

And this, from the *Akron Beacon Journal:*

> He is one of those *athletes who has* a . . .

Or this, from the *Washington Post:*

> He is one of the few *people* in the neighborhood *who ever comes in . . .*

It seems to be widely believed that the subject of the verb in those clauses is singular, but all these examples are incorrect (which you can see at a glance when you look at the clauses in italics). *Mitzi* is not the subject of *hears from her; who* is the subject. And the antecedent of *who* is *people*, a plural noun requiring a plural verb. Mitzi is only one of those *people who hear from her.*

The other two examples should be *athletes who have*, not *athletes who has;* and *people who come in,* not *people who comes in.*

If you're in doubt, reverse the order of the sentence and you will see immediately which verb to use:

> Of the people who hear from her, Mitzi is one.

One more, please, before I drop the subject. This example comes from the *Miami Herald:*

> More than 4.25 inches of rain were reported by mid-morning.

Strange as it may seem to that writer, the correct verb here is *was,* not *were.* To quote from my old grammar book: "A noun denoting a quantity or amount governs a verb in the singular." For example:

> Two gallons of gas is enough to get us home.

> Three cubes of sugar is too much in one cup of tea.

Two and *three* are plural, all right, but here they represent a measurement of an amount and require a singular verb.

Stray Notes

I am indebted to two Washington writers, Dick Ryan and Terry Shea, one for finding and the other passing on this gem, from the *Rockville* (Md.) *Gazette* about the death of a hotel/restaurant magnate:

> I have a hunch he squoze the pimple of life
> for all it was worth. Now you know why
> the food is so delicious at [his] restaurants.

In fairness, I must note that the writer did not originate *squoze;* he had used it earlier in the piece when quoting folksy old Ronald Reagan about a pimple on his nose. But grant the writer a pardon on *squoze,* substitute *squeezed* for it, and the paragraph still stands as a capital offense.

7

=

LET
US
NOT
AVOUCH

=

The foolish and compulsive search for substitutes for good old said. *But sometimes it pays off.*

Some editors with otherwise sound judgment will disagree with what I am about to propound. In truth, I can remember when I was on the other side of this argument myself. But I have given this a lot of study and am now thoroughly convinced: To search compulsively for a substitute for *said* every time you must attribute a statement is to waste time and to risk looking silly in print.

Bear in mind that I do not suggest that you should *never* seek a substitute, that you simply adopt *said* as your standard attributive verb and dismiss the whole matter from your mind. When a person utters something in a particular way, by all means seek a verb that describes the precise way he said it. But to search *compulsively* for a substitute *every time* (those being the key words in my little doctrine) is, I repeat, foolish. For example, look at this, from page one of the *Wall Street Journal:*

> "The timid and fragile don't try the sport,"
> swaggers Bonnie Warner, a fearless, sturdy
> college student.

Now Bonnie may have been swaggering when she said that. But, although the word is in the process of being corrupted, a good dictionary advises that to *swagger* is to "walk with a conceited or lordly strut." Try doing that with your mouth. The writer might have used *boast* or *brag*, both of which can be done with the mouth, but either word might have offended Bonnie. So, while we can all commend the writer for the effort to be vivid, he should have given up at that point and settled for *says*.

Consider this one, from the *Detroit News*. A fellow named Smith has been talking about a loan he negotiated for his company.

> "And the best part about it is that we got it at 8.5 percent," Smith chimed.

He chimed? *Webster II* offers one possibility: "To recite with a musical cadence; to utter singsong." But it's hard to believe there is anything musical or cadent about the words Smith said there. Why not just let him *say* them?

When I discovered that *chimed*, I thought it unique. But I later found this in the *Boston Herald*:

> "Although it was not much more than I had earned 10 years ago, there was no choice but to agree," chimed Chellis.

Here's another odd one, also from the *Detroit News:*

"So," he hoots, "you try to look like you're working."

Did this fellow utter a loud shout, or cry out or shout in contempt, or make a sound resembling that of an owl? It seems improbable.

Another from the *News:*

> Elizabeth Taylor sued an Italian dress company and an advertising agency for unauthorized use of her picture. Miss Taylor indicated $420,000 as minimum compensation.

The picture I get is of Elizabeth Taylor sitting there, lips sealed, while lawyers hold up flash cards, each bearing a dollar figure. To each she shakes her head no. Finally one lawyer holds up a card reading *$420,000.* Miss Taylor smiles and touches a forefinger to the point of her nose. She has indicated. Moral: *Indicate* has its specific uses, but it is not interchangeable with *said* (or, in the example above, *asked for*).

Also from the *News:*

> Kogan refuted Melki's claims that Kogan drew maps for use in the contract killing.
> "Those are maps that Melki drew," Kogan said. "He was trying to show me that he could murder Reva."
> Melki declined to comment.

Newspaper stories often use *refute* as a substitute for *said*, and the excerpt above demonstrates the pitfall. It's clear from the second paragraph that Kogan did not refute Melki's claims; he contradicted or disputed them. To refute is to *prove* something or someone wrong.

You run into similar problems with *explain*, as this example from the *News* illustrates:

> Kirkland explained yesterday that Congress, even the Democratic House, is too conservative and that President Reagan's policies are "doing great damage to the country."

To explain is to clarify an established fact. You can explain how something works or clear up something that is difficult to understand. All Lane Kirkland can do here, however, is explain that *he believes* Congress is too conservative, etc. Even if you agree with his view, it is opinion, not established fact. The writer simply used *explain* as a loose alternative to *said*, and it was wrong.

There is, however, a real problem with *said*. An example from that same story will illustrate:

> He said many of the rank and file have become . . .
> He said 65 percent of the blue collar workers . . .

He said the AFL-CIO wants
candidates . . .

Three consecutive paragraphs opened with *he said*.
That is the problem, but it would not be solved by
substituting alternatives for *said*. It is a writing problem, not a word problem. You see the same thing in
stories that, paragraph after paragraph, give the
source's name, followed by *said* and then the quota-
tion: *John Jones said:* [quote]; *Sam Smith said:*
[quote]; *Mary Roe said:* [quote]. Changing one *said*
to *declared* and another to *asserted* won't relieve the
monotony of that kind of writing. The reader would
still be hammered relentlessly by *said*s (or their substitutes). What is needed is a more imaginative way to
unfold this kind of material.

When the writing is skillful, the word *said* becomes
almost invisible. To test that theory, I cross-sectioned
the work of several noted authors, things I had read
without noticing any surplus of *said*s.

In one chapter of *The Night in Lisbon*, by Erich
Maria Remarque, I found 58 attributive verbs. He used
two *whispers*, two *murmurs*, one *laugh*, one *went on*,
and one *continued*. On all other occasions, he used
said—51 times out of 58. But I hadn't noticed until I
went back and counted.

In the vivid river-crossing scene in *A Farewell to
Arms*, Hemingway had 12 occasions to attribute dia-

log. He used *said* every time. What did he do when writing as a journalist? From his Spanish Civil War reportage, I examined a dispatch from Madrid of April 14, 1937. Once he used a quote followed by *I told him.* Every other time he used *said*—24 times in all. F. Scott Fitzgerald, in a short story called "Magnetism," had 48 opportunities. People cried when, indeed, that was what they did; they exclaimed, or murmured, or whispered in appropriate places. But mostly they just *said* —31 out of 48 times.

You want something more modern? Try the splendid autobiography of Russell Baker, *Growing Up.* For this test, I cut into the book at three points, observing his dialog until each chapter ended. He was required to attribute dialog in 59 places and he used *said* in 50 of them. Somebody roared once, somebody blurted, somebody whispered, but never once did Baker use a substitute just for variety.

That's the key, I think. You seek a better word not for variety or novelty but to report precisely how a person said a thing if he did it in some distinctive way. This from the *Detroit News* will illustrate:

> Dirty Harry/Clint Eastwood is squinting down the barrel of his .357-caliber Magnum.
> "Go ahead," Eastwood aspirates, daring the dude to begin shooting. "Make my day."

Have you seen Eastwood in that scene? That is *exactly* what he does: He aspirates. This writer wasn't seeking a cheap alternative to *says* for variety's sake; he wanted the precise verb that would describe how the man said it. And he found it.

In sum, the search for a better verb—for the right reason—is laudable. When you find it, bravo. But when you don't, don't be ashamed to use just plain *said*.

Before I drop the subject, there's a related problem that needs some attention. On occasion it's necessary to find a way to report what a person says without making it seem that what he says is fact. Example from the *News:*

> In a brief meeting with newsmen in Young's
> office, Mr. Carter called President Reagan's
> economic program a "catastrophe." Citing
> a national unemployment rate of 14 to 17
> percent, with unemployment among blacks
> at 21 percent, Mr. Carter said: ...

I am well aware of the argument that official unemployment rates understate the facts. But *the* unemployment rate is a specific figure, and even at the depth of the recent recession it never even came close to 14–17 percent. That is simply Carter's opinion of what the rate was. To let him *cite* it is improper, because to cite is to call attention to known fact. What

Carter can *say* is that although the official rate is *x* percent, the real rate, in his opinion, is 14 to 17 percent. If he didn't make it clear, the reporter has to make it clear for him.

Note invites similar troubles, illustrated by this from the *News:*

> He noted that Mr. Reagan won the
> presidency by 182,000 votes.

My almanac shows that Reagan won 43,899,248 votes to 35,481,435 for Carter and 5,719,437 for Anderson. If the speaker has some theory about how changing 182,000 votes could have defeated Reagan, fine— let him explain that. But you cannot let him "note" something that is contrary to established fact, any more than you can let me "note" that a pterodactyl is flying by my window just now.

Stray Notes

The lead on a sports story in the *New York Post* advises that the Jets "signed veteran free-agent T Steve August and claimed T Sid Abramowitz off the waiver wire."

Odd, I thought, that both of these players had *T* for a first initial. Later in the story, I read that "rookie LB Troy Benson" had been placed on "IR," and it dawned on me what was going on. This writer was using *T* for *tackle*, *LB* for *linebacker*, *IR* for *injured reserve*, and so on.

Well, I suppose you could argue that a football fan would read that story without pause. (However, I *am* a football fan, but I read my literate sports stories in the *Washington Post* and need no interpreter for them.) That's the same defense a courthouse reporter makes for writing that somebody was indicted for *uttering* and that a defendant *stood mute*. Those are courthouse terms that mean specific things to courthouse habitués. But they mean something else to lay readers, unless explained.

Consider this *New York Times* item, quoted in full:

> Lotus Development Corp., Cambridge,
> Mass., said future versions of its business
> software products, 1-2-3 and Symphony, as
> well as other new products, would be
> encrypted so they could be directly
> installed and booted from hard disks.

Is that any more defensible than sports jargon or legal jargon?

THE
THAT / WHICH
MATTER

And it does matter. Use a which *for a* that *and your readers may have to have their stomachs pumped.*

Happy hour is over, and you have just arrived home from your favorite lounge, where you consumed two perfect manhattans and most of a bowl of ashtolaka nuts. You are leafing idly through a consumer magazine when your eyes fix on the warning:

> If you eat ashtolaka nuts which come from the groves of the Portmanteau Islands, you may die within hours, for they are deadly poison.

What to do? Well, because the author didn't write a sentence with a clear meaning, it's impossible to know whether to proceed blithely to dinner or have your stomach pumped.

Did the author mean that *all* ashtolaka nuts come from the Portmanteau Islands and, therefore, they're all poisonous? Or maybe he meant that ashtolaka nuts from only those particular islands are poisonous, while others are edible. You could read the sentence either way.

Shouldn't there be some way to write that sentence so the reader knows exactly what it means? There should be, and there is. But the writer would have to know the difference between a restrictive and a non-restrictive clause to make the meaning clear—perhaps not too much to ask of someone who holds himself out to be a writer.

I bring this up because a number of writers and editors have asked me if I could clarify the difference between *that* and *which*. I contrived that ashtolaka example to show that the difference is not just pedantic daintiness, but can be crucial.

But forget ashtolaka nuts for the moment. I'll try to sort them out later. Right now, let's make a frontal assault on the *that/which* problem, the problem of restrictive and nonrestrictive clauses. Consider this simple sentence:

The 1983-model cars will cost more money.

No clause at all there, restrictive or nonrestrictive, and the meaning is clear: All 1983-model cars will cost more money.

But suppose we wanted to add some incidental information about those cars, just sort of by-the-bye, while writing the sentence. We might write:

The 1983-model cars, *which will get better mileage*, will cost more money.

Still the same basic sentence, but in a *parenthetical* way, we have added a piece of information about the cars. We could stick that clause in or leave it out, and the meaning of the sentence would remain the same: All 1983-model cars will cost more.

The italic clause did not restrict the meaning of the sentence to any particular kinds of cars. Therefore, it is a nonrestrictive clause. By rule of grammar, it is set off by commas—it is parenthetical, I repeat. And it begins with a *which*, not a *that*.

Now let's suppose that what we wanted to write was that *some* (but not all) new cars will cost more. We want to specify what cars will cost more. We want to restrict our meaning to just those cars. We might write:

> The 1983-model cars *that get better mileage than their 1982 counterparts* will cost more money.

Now this is an entirely different sentence. Here we are not just adding information that is incidental to the meaning of the sentence. It is *essential* to the meaning, not parenthetical. The italic clause restricts the statement to only certain kinds of cars. Therefore, it is a restrictive clause. It must be introduced with *that*, not *which*, and it must *not* be set off by commas.

Suppose the sentence read:

> The 1983-model cars *which get better
> mileage than their 1982 counterparts* will
> cost more money.

No commas around the clause. Yet it is introduced by *which*. Confusion sets in. What does the sentence mean? Hard to tell, the way the clause is introduced and punctuated. You have to guess at its meaning. You can't tell whether the clause restricts the meaning to certain cars only or whether all new cars will cost more.

I'll grant that sometimes a reader can divine the meaning from the context. But why should he have to divine the meaning? Why can't he read a sentence and know in a millisecond exactly what it means, without having to pause and figure it out?

And sometimes the meaning is not at all clear from the context. As the ashtolaka example illustrates, the *that/which* matter can have grave consequences if the meaning is unclear.

Returning, then, to ashtolaka, let's assume the author wanted to warn us *only* about nuts from the Portmanteau Islands. He wanted to restrict the meaning of the sentence to nuts from those islands. What he wanted, then, was a restrictive clause—something essential to the sentence, not parenthetical. He could have accomplished what he intended by writing:

> If you eat ashtolaka nuts *that come from
> the groves of the Portmanteau Islands,* you
> may die within hours.

Note that the clause is not set off by commas and it begins with *that*. So punctuated and so introduced, it is a restrictive clause, restricting the meaning to nuts from those islands. Those and only those are poisonous.

But if the author meant that *all* ashtolaka nuts are poisonous, he wanted a nonrestrictive clause, introduced by *which* and set off by parenthetical commas:

> If you eat ashtolaka nuts, *which come from the groves of the Portmanteau Islands*, you may die within hours.

The clause in italics is nonrestrictive. It does not restrict the meaning to certain nuts only. The sentence means that if you eat *any* ashtolaka nuts, you will die. It also offers the incidental information that the nuts come from the Portmanteau Islands. If you remove the parenthetical clause, the sentence still means the same.

That is the key to whether you have a restrictive or nonrestrictive clause. If it can be removed without changing the meaning of the sentence, then the information is only incidental, not essential, to the sentence. As a nonrestrictive clause, it should be introduced with a *which* and set off with commas (think of them as shrunken parentheses). But if the clause is essential to the meaning of the sentence, it restricts the meaning. Therefore, it is a restrictive clause: It should be introduced with *that* and should not be set off with commas.

Although these rules are violated daily, they are not really hard to learn. After a few minutes of concentration almost anybody can grasp the principle involved. Then a few days of discipline, applied every time you have to deal with a *that* or a *which*, will have you making the right choice automatically.

During those early days of struggle it might help to keep William Ross Wallace's familiar line in mind:

> The hand *that rocks the cradle* is the hand
> *that rules the world*.

Two clauses, both restrictive. Both essential to the meaning of the sentence. Neither set off by commas because the information isn't parenthetical. Both introduced by *that*. Think how that line would read if the clauses were nonrestrictive:

> The hand, *which rocks the cradle*, is the
> hand, *which rules the world*.

The *which*es and the commas would mean that the clauses are supposed to be nonrestrictive (nonessential to the meaning of the sentence). But try removing both clauses. What you have left is absurd: *The hand is the hand*. Obviously both clauses are essential and should not be set off by commas.

You probably have noted that both restrictive and nonrestrictive clauses can begin with *who*. No problem. The principle is the same. Keep in mind the example cited by Strunk and White in *The Elements of Style:*

> People *who live in glass houses* shouldn't
> throw stones.

The clause introduced by *who* is clearly essential to the meaning; it is restrictive. Remove it and the meaning changes. Set the clause off with commas (or parentheses) and see what it means.

But in this next sentence, the clause is nonrestrictive, not essential to the meaning:

> The winning candidate, *who had never run
> for office before*, proved to be a crook and
> a dope fiend.

The clause contains only parenthetical information, so it is set off by commas.

Well, enough. I have labored the point, I know, but I did it deliberately. The point *seems* so hard to drive home. I know writers who say they have read and reread various explanations and still can't figure it out. I know others who can't figure it out and so try to pretend it isn't important.

I once had an editor who changed some of my *that*s to *which*es, some *which*es to *that*s, with no apparent reason. When I asked why, he said he couldn't understand the difference. So if I had written *that* the last time, he would change the next *that* to *which*, carefully alternating them as if they were interchangeable.

He left the newspaper business shortly thereafter and went to work for the Chamber of Commerce.

Stray Notes

===

It may not be an imminent national catastrophe, but I'd like to fly a small warning flag about the word *each*. If not carefuly watched, it can dig a writer into a deep hole. Note this one, from the *Wall Street Journal:*

> Harry Hoiles, his sister and descendants of their deceased brother Clarence each owns one-third of the company and has four seats on the board.

The orderly mind reels at that sentence. How many thirds are there? How many seats on the board? Oh, you can trace back through it and figure out what the writer was trying to say, but he wasn't trying very hard. He could have written:

> Harry Hoiles and his sister own one third of the company each, and each has four seats on the board. Descendants of their deceased brother, Clarence, own the other third and have four seats.

From the *Detroit News:*

> The Lions' home stadium, which seats
> 80,638, stands to lose about $275,000 a game
> for each game not played.

If this writer had maintained an *each* alert, he might have caught the redundancy.

Nothing wrong with *each*, of course. But when it appears before you, better look both ways to make sure nothing else is coming.

9

FOWLER,
FOLLETT,
ET AL.

Why you must own Fowler, and how not *to use it. Other books a writer needs.*

What reference books would help you improve as a writer or editor?

Without doubt, the writer's best friend is *Modern English Usage*, by H. W. Fowler. (It is now available in paperback.) Anybody who is serious about writing or editing should own this book *and use it frequently*.

Now a few things need to be said about Fowler.

Occasionally, upon learning that the book's full title is *A Dictionary of Modern English Usage*, some rube will protest, "But I already have a dictionary"—thus displaying his ignorance of Fowler. Fowler is not a dictionary like *Webster II* or the *American Heritage*. It is not a book to keep on the shelf until you need to check a spelling or a definition. It must be studied.

Oh, you can look up some words in it. If you turn to *luxuriant*, for example, Fowler will define the difference between *luxuriant* and *luxurious:*

> *Luxurious* is the adjective that belongs in sense to *luxury* and conveys the ideas of comfort or delight or indulgence; *luxuriant*

> has nothing to do with these, implying only
> rich growth, vigorous shooting forth,
> teeming, prolific . . .

Modern English Usage is called a dictionary because its entries are arranged in alphabetical order. An entry may be simply a word with its proper pronunciation or an amusing little essay about some point of usage.

For example, if you look up *massive*, which should be a daily penance for many writers and editors, you will find this entry (here shortened):

> *Massive* in its figurative sense is a useful and
> expressive word to be treated with respect
> and discrimination. The virtue is being
> taken out of it now that it has become a
> vogue word, ousting more ordinary and
> often more suitable adjectives. Almost
> every day's newspapers will provide
> evidence of its popularity.

Fowler offers examples of the overuse of *massive*, but why quote those when there are plenty of examples in our current newspapers? I pick up the *Los Angeles Times* and find four *massive*s in three adjoining stories on page one: *damage is massive, the material toll was massive, massive demonstrations*, and *massively unbalanced federal budget*. And in a sectional front page inside the same issue: *massive amounts of travel*. In the same newspaper, two days later: *massive logistical operation* and *massive development*. In the state of Washington, the *Spokesman Review and Spokane Chronicle* speaks of a *massive citizens lawsuit.* The *San Francisco Examiner* reports *massive debts,* and the (Portland) *Oregonian* tells of a *massive wiretapping operation.* A single *Washington Post* story of only six paragraphs contains *a massive campaign* and *massive remodeling.* The *Post* also reports that a traffic victim *died instantly of massive head injuries.* Now, if I read that somebody died instantly of head injuries, I think I can safely assume the injuries were more than a mere annoyance; I don't need to be told they were massive.

Looking back, I see that I heralded Fowler's essays as amusing, and perhaps the *massive* entry fell short of that. Here's a better example:

> Hackneyed phrases. . . . There are
> thousands for whom the only sound sleep
> is the sleep of the just, the light at dusk
> must always be dim; all beliefs are
> cherished, all confidence is implicit, all
> ignorance blissful, all isolation splendid. . . .
> The witty gentleman who equipped
> coincidence with her long arm has doubtless
> suffered . . . at seeing that arm so mercilessly
> overworked.

Another thing that needs to be explained about Fowler is how not to use it. The book is fascinating for anyone who likes words, but it is not a novel. If you buy the book and swear that, by golly, you're going to read it this weekend, you will abandon the cause long before reaching page 725. One Detroit writer told me he always intended to read Fowler, but hadn't touched it since he bought it 15 years ago. It was just too much to tackle.

That's just not the way to go about it—at least, it isn't for me. I browse in Fowler. In fact, in periods of insomnia, I get Fowler off the shelf and let it fall open wherever it will. I start reading there and by pursuing cross-references suddenly discover I have been reading for 45 minutes or so. I can't attest that it's soporific, but over the years I've digested a lot of Fowler that way. Even if you're not an insomniac, the free-fall is still a good approach to Fowler. In an odd half hour or so, while you're waiting for the next event on your schedule, let the book fall open and see where it leads.

Suppose, for example, it opens to the *-tion* entry. At the end of Fowler's little discourse, you find this cross-reference: "See also *Abstractitis*," an essay in which Fowler says, "this disease [is] now endemic on both sides of the Atlantic." Because the *abstractitis* entry is both witty and useful, you probably will read it to the end, where you will find cross-references to *periphrasis*, *membership*, *tautology*, and *-tion* words.

Fine essays all, and any writer who took just that one dose of Fowler (and heeded his words) would find himself a better writer for it. Tap into the book two or three times a week, over the years, and you will infuse Fowler into your veins painlessly, until he becomes part of your own writer's conscience.

A good companion to Fowler is Wilson Follett's *Modern American Usage* (Hill & Wang). It's not the equal of Fowler, but then I know of nothing that is. Follett is also arranged in dictionary form.

I approach Follett as I do Fowler, browsing in odd moments—and, of course, looking up specific entries as needed. Just to give you some of the flavor of Follett, here's part of his essay on journalese:

> In general, the tone of journalese is the tone of contrived excitement. When the facts by themselves do not make the reader's pulse beat faster, the journalist thinks it is his duty to apply the spur and whip of breathless words and phrases. Since these exist only in finite numbers they get repeated, and repetition begets their weakening, their descent into journalese. That is how we have worn out the epithets *drastic*, *crucial*, *essential*, *crushing*, *bitter*, *ironic*, and others that a studied writer will use only with caution.

The Handbook of Good English by Edward D. Johnson, recently published by Facts on File Publications, is outstanding. It may not be as much fun as Fowler, but its just as important.

Words Into Type by M. Skillen and R. Gay (Prentice-Hall Inc., 1974) contains good sections on word usage and grammar, and if you don't own a separate grammar book, this one will do. In the word section, you'll find a handy list showing which preposition to use with which noun, verb, or adjective. (It's *oblivious of*, for example, not *to*.) There's also a ready reference for words often confused (*blatant* and *flagrant*, *career* and *careen*, *flaunt* and *flout*).

As for a grammar book, I survived for years without one, a foolish part of my bullheaded rebellion against a few pedantic English teachers. Along the way, however, I mellowed a bit and began to see the need for a good grammar text that could solve the occasional problem that would pop up. So I bought *Proper Words in Proper Places* by J. O. Bailey. That may be out of print, but there must be others. As a sinner saved, I urge you to buy one. (But leaf through it first to make sure it's written in English.)

Finally, I must mention *The Elements of Style* by Strunk and White. Everybody knows about it, of course, but if I didn't mention it, someone might take the omission as tacit disapproval of this excellent little book. *Elements* should be in every writer's possession.

But this book is for reading, not browsing. And rereading. And rereading. Hell, it's no bigger than a quark. You could study it thoroughly about four times a year and never miss the time. What its distilled wisdom can do for your writing is immeasurable, if you put your heart into it.

Stray Notes

You can argue that it's idiomatic, that the words should not be taken literally—but it irks and distracts me nonetheless. I'm talking about a common usage that turns certainty into speculation, as in this caption under a photo of Geoffrey Holder dresses in the handsome *Architectural Digest:*

> Holder's costume designs for *The Wiz* may
> have won him a Tony, but his favorite
> client is still his wife.

Now, it is a verifiable fact that Holder's costume designs for *The Wiz* won him a Tony (he got one for directing it too). *Architectural Digest* knows that. Then what is this "*may* have won" business?

What's wrong with just saying it straight?

> Holder's costume designs for *The Wiz* won
> him a Tony, but his favorite client is still
> his wife.

Even a publication that chooses to call a rolltop desk a *bureau à cylindre* could have written the caption that way, I think, without offending its refined readers.

INTERVIEWING MR. EASTER BUNNY

—
—

Adventures in "creativity" lead some writers into embarrassing stunts. Watching yourself go by.

To hear them tell it, writers are an oppressed people. They struggle to make their stories sparkle, but their editors, lacking imagination, strip their work of everything fresh. The editors just won't let them be creative.

So, to the perpetual question: Should editors permit writers to be creative, to seek ways to make their writing distinctive? Well, certainly, you may reply.

In my mind, there's no neat answer. Creativity is so amorphous. One writer's creativity can be another writer's ipecac. What is inventive and creative to one writer can strike another as strained and artificial. Some writers may think that to be creative is to use very large words in very complicated sentences.

Thus we are on marshy ground when a writer feels a surge of creativity and an editor has to judge the result. His decision comes down to two essentials, I think: Taste and effectiveness.

Let's take effectiveness first.

A good technician can make a piece effective, no matter how unorthodox his approach. That is, he can make certain that it meets all the requirements for good communication: It instantly seizes the reader's attention; it sustains interest; its meaning is unmistakable; and the facts it seeks to convey are easily discernible as facts.

An editor has a right and duty to insist on these essentials. The space in a newspaper is not the sole property of the writer, to fill as he alone sees fit. (Not even a columnist has *absolute* control over a piece of space.)

To look at it another way, a free-spirited baseball player might want to put a little creativity into the unvarying, ageless routine of running the bases. Perhaps he wants to skip or cartwheel instead of run— something inventive that's sure to win attention. But he tries it and is thrown out at first on what could have been a stand-up double. His effort is not effective. So his manager, the stodge, forbids him to be creative.

Or a rookie pitcher's deportment on the mound is so distinctive that he delights the fans, who flock to the ballpark, in turn delighting the club owner. Still, he is required to pitch the ball into a precise space. If he can't do that, even his distinctive style won't save him from baseball oblivion. He has failed to be effective.

Judging a piece of writing for effectiveness is not such a tough call. Judging it for taste, however, is. Even if an inventive approach qualifies as effective, it still must pass the taste test.

By taste, of course, I'm not suggesting a test of whether the piece is coarse or obscene. I mean, whether the piece succeeds is a matter of individual taste. The author may think it's cute as hell and that people will stop him on the street to compliment him on a great piece of writing. Somebody will (the author's mother, for one), no matter how much the piece smells. As humorist Mort Sahl said, there are so many people out there, somebody will dig anything. But if readers of reasonable intelligence and tolerance find the piece juvenile, or cutesy, or nauseating, then it has failed the taste test. It embarrasses the whole publication and, I'll wager, will embarrass the writer some years later.

So a writer may be pleased with his bravura performance, finding it to his own taste. But he may encounter a fellow writer or an editor who finds it hard to believe that the author actually produced this work and, what's more, wants to let the world see it. Whose sense of taste should prevail?

In my time I have tried unorthodox approaches now and then. Some of them worked, and I enjoyed the compliments that followed. But some of them didn't, and I thank the Fates for the friends and editors who told me so before I made a fool of myself.

I recall one such effort, an attempt to write a story about the windfall profits tax as if I were one of Dashiell Hammett's operatives reporting to the home office. As I wrote, it seemed to be working, so I saw it through. Then, however, I began to doubt. Did I really bring it off? I kept rereading, but I couldn't tell. I decided to ship it off to my editor, who telephoned the next day and in a sad (or was it wary?) voice told me the thing "just didn't work." He got no argument from me. Not a word. His judgment was all I needed to confirm my own grave doubts. Thank heaven for him.

On the other hand, suppose I had felt certain that I had produced a winner—as I have felt on occasion. Then I would have argued with him. His judgment still would have prevailed, of course, but my argument at least would have tested his judgment that the story didn't work. This mutual testing is important.

What was I really trying to do when I wrote that piece? Why does a writer try to write a story as if it were a diary entry, a three-act play, or a memo to his editor (often called, in these efforts, "the man in the green eye shade")? Reflecting on my own motives, I conclude that writers who use those gimmicks primarily seek to call attention to themselves. Communication is secondary. That's not an accusation; it's a confession.

I am reminded of one of the admonitions in the old *New York Herald*'s "Don't List": "Do not compose a story so that the reader feels that the writer was watching himself go by. The highest art is that which conceals art."

Now, having condemned myself and others for these excesses, let me at least glance in the other direction.

I believe it takes some courage for a writer to try an unorthodox way of telling a story. The risk of failure —and of ridicule—is high. Many writers would rather play it safe every time, writing everything the routine way. And some editors, not wishing to risk criticism for approving an unorthodoxy, may automatically quash every attempt the writers make until finally they despair and stop trying. Life is so much easier that way, and the editor never has to admit his inability to judge whether the story works.

I admire the writer who asks himself, frequently, the simple question, What is the best way to do this *particular* story? Rather than fit everything into one of the standard forms, he dares to examine the *particular* circumstances to see if there's a better way to go about this story. That kind of examination will not often (or so I hope) lead to an interview with Mr. Easter Bunny, a Dear Diary entry, a Dear Boss memo, or some other conceit. But if the writer, exercising his self-restraint, does conclude there is a different and better way to do the piece, he should try it, relying on his own and his editor's taste to tell him whether it's really roses he is smelling or skunk cabbage.

And, in turn, the editor should not approach these efforts with a closed mind, automatically suppressing them all and demonstrating to all hands that nothing out of the ordinary will ever be tolerated. ("Get out of here," says the editor to Don Marquis. "You're going to pretend that a cockroach climbed up on the keyboard and typed this story?") I think a good editor welcomes signs that his writers are always trying, always stretching themselves—that they haven't fallen into a numb acceptance of the dull and commonplace.

Still, I hope that the writer who strives to be distinctive will do it not just with gaudy stunts or acrostic sentences but by tirelessly working to transform the abstract into the concrete, by squeezing out the excess, by making clarity and precision his constant goals.

I like this piece of advice, which is so apt here that you might suspect me of making it up for the occasion (I didn't). Flaubert is said to have counseled Maupassant: "Never have recourse to tricks, however happy; or to buffooneries of language, to avoid a difficulty. This is the way to become original."

Stray Notes

I know of no category for the kind of foolishness I'm about to decry here, but it needs decrying:

From the *New York Post*:

> Dale Olson said Hudson told his friends that if he was going to die, he wanted more than anything to go out helping others.
>
> "He felt that if he was going to die, then he wanted to help others," . . . said Olson.

What is the sense of telling us something in indirect quotes and following it immediately with a direct quote saying the same thing? You hear that often on broadcast news. The newscaster tells us that John Jones says he ran across the street when he heard the blast and found the wounded man. Then we hear a tape of John Jones saying: "I ran across the street when I heard the blast and found the wounded man." Once is enough.

BEFORE YOU START TO WRITE

=

The nutshell summary and the outline: how they structure a story and help avoid writer's block.

At the start of all this, when I was displaying examples of writing sins, I promised that eventually I would stop nagging about things *not* to do and turn instead to things *to* do. My theory was that one's writing could be improved considerably by eliminating the negative; then would come the time to move to another level.

I think that time has come. I will now suggest one way to attack a problem that many writers face: how to organize a piece before you start to write it.

Many writers will contend, with all honesty, that they have no problem with organization, and no doubt some of them are right. Others who believe they have no problem, however, continue to be mystified when their material is rejected or completely rewritten. Bad structure—or no structure—is a felony often unrecognized by the perpetrator.

Still others resist all advice to structure their stories. That's writing to formula, they sniff, stifling my creativity; I want my individuality to show. Well, that's nonsense. When we talk about structure, we're talking about no more than the skeleton of a story. How it is fleshed out can be as creative and brilliant as your genius can make it. Anatomically speaking, we all have skeletons, but we don't all look alike. Paul Newman and I are about the same age and height, but nobody, in all my life, has ever asked if he could have my autograph, please, Mr. Newman.

Another caveat before we proceed: The technique I am about to explain is not necessary in, and will not work for, some kinds of writing. Fiction, for example. And it will be clear at once that here we are *not* talking about standard newspaper stories. For some pieces, the writer may find it undesirable or even unwise to use this kind of structure. Impressionistic writing comes to mind. Or in a profile you may not wish to put horns or halo on the subject; just paint the picture and let the reader judge for himself. (See the classic *Portrait of Hemingway* by Lillian Ross, published originally in *The New Yorker* and later as a book by Simon & Schuster.) Even so, whatever you are writing needs *some* kind of structure, if not the kind I am suggesting.

The essential first step is to write *for yourself* a brief statement explaining precisely what your story is— its major point. All that you have learned adds up to . . . what? It is not enough that you know the story is about crime. *What* about crime? What is the central theme of your story? This statement of theme must really be nailed to the deck. A reader should be able to finish your piece and say to a companion, "This story says that . . ." and relate the theme of the story. If the reader doesn't understand that clearly, the story has failed. It has failed because you didn't understand the theme yourself before you started to write.

In fact, I have discovered that many times when I thought I was ready to write, I immediately ran into writer's block—before I could put down a word. The trouble usually was that I didn't really understand the point of my story. Oh, sure, my mind was filled with many interviews and facts, but I had not stopped to ask and answer the question, What is the point of this story? So I would, almost simplemindedly, write myself a memo. It would begin, "This is a story that says . . ." And in a few typewritten lines I would write what amounted to a nutshell summary of the story, including not only the main theme but any subthemes essential to a faithful summary. I usually found that this forced me to think my way through the materials and put everything in focus; the writer's block would evaporate, and I could proceed.

But the purpose of the nutshell summary is not just to order your own thinking. This summary, perhaps refined a bit, will become the reader's focus in the story too. The summary will appear early in your piece. It may even turn out to be the lead paragraph, if the theme itself is dramatic enough to seize the reader and lure him on. Or you may have some brief bit of color or action to serve that purpose, after which you quickly tie into your summary.

Nearly 30 years ago, when I was marveling at the things the *Wall Street Journal* was doing on its front page (but before I had any idea that I would ever work there), I came into possession of an interesting memo. It was written by some *WSJ* editor for internal instruction. It was no fancy thing. It was marked up with inserts and blacked-out words. The heading on it was "Style Pattern for Page One News-Features," and it explained how to do them. (Anyone familiar with the *Wall Street Journal* knows that these front-page stories are not at all like standard news stories appearing in a conventional newspaper.)

This was a key point in that memo:

> These page-one "leaders," as we call them, are interpretive stories. They most often report trends—what they mean and what they portend. . . . The stories generally have one theme or point. This is usually put into a one- or two-paragraph nutshell summary high up in the story.

That's a fundamental part of much expository writing today, whether it's a magazine piece, an essay, a speech, whatever. So write it first.

Next, make a list of all the essential elements you will have to cover to support the theme of your nutshell summary—in the order you believe you should write them. You may decide, on reflection, to juggle the order; it would be more logical, you may conclude, to deal with Topic E before Topic C. This is the time to juggle, not after you have written your way knee-deep into the jungle.

Now, under Topic A list the materials you have that explain A. Make the same kind of list under B, and so on. (You may have noticed that I have not used the word *outline* here; it spooks some people. But in effect that is what we are creating.)

I think it's a good idea then to arrange your materials in piles or stacks—everything pertaining to A in one pile, to B in another, etc. If possible, cut up your notes into pieces so that everything about A can be separated and stacked in your A pile. If your notes are physically inseparable, you can go through them with different-colored pens so that every A note is identified by a red mark, for example, B by blue, or whatever colors turn you on. (This is especially satisfying if you happen to be a felt-pen freak.)

Whatever Mickey Mouse system you use to collate, the point of this exercise is to cut down the amount of time you waste, while writing, to hunt down that elusive fact or quote that you know "has to be in this mess somewhere." Nothing will shut off the creative juices faster than an hour of hair-pulling as you search for the statistic or statement you need right now.

Now, one more list. I learned this from Henry Gemmill, whose writing I admired so much. His stories were sprinkled throughout with bits of color, descriptive phrases, little anecdotes, and illustrative quotes that whisked the reader right through to the end of the piece. I knew you were supposed to do that, but I wondered how he did it so well. The trick, he told me, was to make a separate list of all these color items as he went through his materials, before he started to write. He would parallel this color list with his list of major elements, roughly following the same order. He might even draw lines from items in the color list to items in the major list, showing where he thought a color item might be put to appropriate use. As he used the color items in writing, he would cross them off. If there were any left when he finished, he tried to find places to work them in. His pieces were little works of art, but behind the art he did a lot of brick masonry.

One more thing before you start to write. This is a good time to decide how you'll end the piece. Maybe you can find a nugget of a quote that sums up the theme in vivid language. Maybe you return to the bit of business you selected for the lead, perhaps with a different twist. (Please, though, spare the reader yet another summation that begins, *But one thing is certain . . .*) Whatever you use, you need a planned ending, so as you go through your materials in the prewriting stage, it's a good idea to spot something and reserve it then and there for your ending.

To recapitulate, this is *one* technique for writing a

story that involves multiple sources, multiple ideas. The steps are:

1. Write a nutshell summary of the theme of the piece, with all its *on-the-other-hands*, its *howevers*, etc. The summary covers all the major elements of the story.

2. Make a list of all the major elements you know you will have to deal with in the story, juggling if necessary to get the items in what you decide is the proper order. Under each topic heading, list the materials you have that support each topic theme.

3. Make a parallel list of bits of description, color, quotes, and so on, so these reader aids are not forgotten during the writing.

4. Physically arrange your materials—all your notes, quotes, documents—in different stacks, one for Topic A, one for B, and so on.

5. Decide how you will end the piece, reserving some appropriate quote or fact to conclude it.

Now you're ready to write.

And if you think writing to structure is mechanical and uncreative, just remember that a sonnet has a very precise structure: 14 lines, no more, no less. But a mechanic named Shakespeare did rather well with it.

Stray Notes

My thanks to Sandra Rubin Tessler, a Detroit writer, for sending me this gem from—I hate to admit it—the *Wall Street Journal* (in a front-page leader):

> One-stop shopping is gone forever, and with the Bell System breaking up, will never return.

My wife found this one in the *Olney* (Md.) *Courier-Gazette:*

> If you want to see your kids' eyes light up and give out with little squeals, then take them to Olney Park and head for the lake.

And then straight to the ophthalmologist.

ON TO
THE MUSE

=

The first paragraph is crisis time. How and why you must use it to lure readers over the interest deadline.

Now you're ready to write, as I said near the close of the last chapter; all the preparatory steps advocated there are done, along with, perhaps, a bow to the muse. So here we go.

You need no hotshot writing consultant to tell you that the first chore you face is the opening paragraph. Evidently, though (as we shall see shortly), there is some need to discuss what a lead paragraph is and what the writer's responsibility in the lead is.

The late Bernard Kilgore used to quote the adage, "the easiest thing for a reader to do is to stop reading." That's wrong, Kilgore would say; the easiest thing to do is to never *start* reading.

So the writer's responsibility in the first paragraph is to do everything that's legal to lure the reader into the piece. If you don't hook him with the very first words, you have lost him. He will never know what sparkling prose you are about to uncork for him, because the reader will never get there unless you make him cross the interest deadline.

That phrase, "cross the interest deadline," is not mine. It is H. A. Overstreet's, and his analysis of why a reader either crosses the deadline or stops reading can be found in his book *Influencing Human Behavior* (W. W. Norton).

I urge everybody to read the appropriate chapter in that book, but experience tells me that few will, so I'll try to summarize his points. The chapter begins:

> There is, in all communication—written or spoken—a certain deadline of interest. If we can cross that deadline we have the world with us—temporarily at least. If we cannot cross it, we may as well retire. The world will have none of us.

Skilled novelists, dramatists, advertisers, and essayists know how to cross the deadline, Overstreet says.

> Unquestionably, they have a way of luring us on. . . . They have the art of stirring us out of our mental sluggishness and carrying us along with them wherever they will. Obviously, no writer without something of this art can hope to be widely successful.

How do they do it? Overstreet studied their work and offers these suggestions:

1. *Start with situations.* "Note how the skilled dramatist [he cites Ibsen] instantly, at the rise of a curtain, creates a situation." Not just words, not abstract ideas, but a situation. Marcel Proust,

he notes, began *Swann's Way* "not with general observations, but with a concrete, easily visualized, and interesting situation."

2. *Start with something that makes a difference.* Let the reader see that the thing about to be discussed will cause something significant, or at least interesting.

3. *Begin with an effect needing a cause.* "If a savage hears a leaf rustle, he is alert. 'What did that?' If we find a large box in our room [that] was previously not there, we are suddenly aroused. 'Who put that there?' 'Who was in the room?' . . . Wherever an effect is presented without its adequate cause, we have what might be called a dynamic form of vacuum. . . . The mind of the reader or hearer is at once alert to fill the causal emptiness with adequate explanation." If you raise a question in the readers' minds, they are forced to read on.

4. *Present a conflict.* Conflict is the essence of drama.

In sum, crossing the interest deadline "is not the result of some vague and mystical 'dramatic' power possessed by a few fortunate individuals," Overstreet says, but "is the result of doing one or more of a few very simple things."

These things must be done, of course, no matter what you're writing. The reader must be hooked quickly by using the most arresting fact or situation you can find in your material. And the *first words*—not just the whole sentence—must work toward that end.

For example, you don't feel as if you had been grabbed when you read a lead like this one, from the *Dallas Morning News:*

> A state court decision by Judge Robert Montgomery has denied the summary judgment motion of Greg Jones and upheld a District 9-AAAAA Executive Committee ruling that the Highland Park senior is ineligible to play football.

Thirty-one lifeless words before we get to some action: *ineligible to play football.* Better to write about the result first and explain the process later.

Not quite so offensive, but close, is this example of a dull lead, from the *New York Times:*

> New Jersey's Education Commissioner today upheld an administrative law judge's order that a 15-year-old girl be allowed on the football team at North Hunterdon High School this fall.

And this one, from the *Philadelphia Inquirer:*

> New Jersey Agriculture Commissioner Arthur Brown Jr. announced yesterday that one case of equine encephalitis had been confirmed in Atlantic County, and he urged

> horse owners to have their animals
> vaccinated against the virus.

Too many newspaper stories begin that way, with a cumbersome title, a name, and—at last—some action. The writer here had something of considerable importance to convey, but the reader has to hack his way to it. To get the interesting fact first, it's sometimes worth it to sacrifice the active voice and adopt the passive (although, as a general rule, the active is preferable).

To illustrate, a *Detroit News* story about the discovery of a skeleton began:

> The skeleton of a sailor who died 63 years
> ago yesterday in a collision of two ore boats
> was found by scuba divers some 230 feet
> under the surface of Lake Superior.

The interesting thing here is *skeleton*, not *scuba divers*, so the writer chose a passive lead to put his best fact forward. *Skeleton* has intrinsic human interest; it is also an effect needing a cause.

Another lead from the *Detroit News:*

> The attorney representing Donald L.
> D—— says he intends to obtain a court
> injunction to prevent "repeated
> harassment" by lawmen in their search for
> D——'s wife.

The story is full of fascinating material, including good quotes the writer got from D——. It turns out that D—— is upset because the police just dug up his backyard in a vain search for clues. But all of that is introduced by *The attorney representing . . .* , a bland and uninviting lead that will turn the reader away in a hurry.

Here's another:

> R. P. Scherer Corp., of Troy, announced that its board of directors unanimously opposed a bid by FMC Corp. of Chicago to buy all of Scherer's stock at prices ranging from $18 to $22 a share in cash or securities.

A good takeover fight, with pocketbook significance to a lot of people, seems to be brewing here, but the first 13 words—the critical words—go by before there's any hint of action. It takes a determined reader to get through that lead.

Another one like it:

> The board of directors of McLouth Steel Corp. received a conditional proposal from Tang Industries Inc. for the purchase of all of McLouth's land, buildings, equipment and certain other assets.

Count the number of bland words you have to read to get to the good part.

(Incidentally, note that in two of these three examples, the first word is *the*. Some people argue that you should *never* begin with *the* or *a*, but I won't go that far. Certainly, if the first sentence should be arresting, then it follows that the first word of that sentence is even more important. And *the* and *a* are neutral words. But I glance at the bookshelves behind me and I see *The Gathering Storm, The Lost Crusade, The Fall of Rome, The Ends of Power, The Price of Power,* and on and on. Book publishers like to sell books; if a first-word *the* is fatal, why would so many titles begin that way? My view is that while I will make a serious effort to avoid starting with *the*, I'll use it if that turns out to be the best way I can find to begin.)

Here's a front-page lead from the *Detroit News* that seemed short (19 words) and to the point:

> Ford Motor Co. plans to begin negotiations
> for the sale of its Rouge Steel operations to
> a Japanese buyer.

Not bad, but it also provides an example of how a lead paragraph can be whittled to make it even better. Why have Ford plan *to begin negotiations for the sale?* That really means that Ford plans to sell the thing, as indeed the headline writer concluded: *Ford readies sale of Rouge steel plant to Japanese.* So we can whack out that phrase and make the lead read:

> Ford Motor Co. plans to sell its Rouge Steel
> operations to a Japanese buyer.

But we can trim some more. Why *operations?* That's an abstract, fuzzy word. Can we find something a bit more concrete? Well, the map accompanying the story uses *steel mill*. That's good enough for me. So we say *mill* instead of *operations*, getting a precise, one-syllable word in place of a long, uncertain one.

Is there more we can do? A still closer look tells us there is. Whom does Ford plan to sell the mill to? The lead says *a Japanese buyer*. But if Ford is the seller, obviously the entity that buys it is a buyer, without our having to say so. So we can replace that unnecessary word with another fact, producing:

> Ford Motor Co. plans to sell its Rouge Steel
> mill to a Japanese steelmaker.

Now we have an even terser lead (14 words instead of 19) and one more fact than the original had. And we cut out two -*tion* words, always a laudable achievement.

All of the examples cited here were from straight news stories, where getting the action or the event to the fore as quickly as possible is usually sufficient. But the same principle—that the first paragraph is an interest deadline that must be crossed—applies as well to nonnews leads.

I know it's not good form to quote one's self, but here is what I wrote on this subject in a memo to the staff of the *National Observer*, where I spent some years, and I see no point in trying to rewrite it:

The function of our opening sentence or paragraph is to seize the reader and entice him to read on—not necessarily to tell him anything yet. Still, the opening paragraph must do more than simply seize his interest —we could do that by writing a series of four-letter words in boldface caps. In addition to seizing his attention, we must give him some clue to what the article is about. . . .

Actually, the real "lead," or the most important thing we have to say, might appear several sentences later in the story, when we have properly prepared the reader to receive this intelligence. It's like a ruffle of drums or a flourish of trumpets before an important announcement is made.

What we need is a bit of business, a dash of color, a setting of the scene—anything that has a direct bearing on what we are about to say, but that provides the reader with a sense of action, of drama, of conflict, or a mental image, or a historical setting.

One thing that sometimes works when I'm preparing to write an intro is to contemplate how television might picture this subject. By making it possible for the audience to see as well as hear the story, TV doubles its sensory appeal. A writer can't duplicate that feat, but he can come close by examining his material to see what he can write about to create mental images for the reader. If you could actually show him a picture, as TV does, what scene would you show? All right, write about that; describe the scene with enough concrete detail that the reader can picture it himself. (And if you can invoke familiar smells and sounds, so much the better. Use all the senses you can.)

I know of no better newspaper practitioners of this art than *Wall Street Journal* writers. Look at their lead paragraphs in those two outside columns on the front page and the story in column 4. Almost invariably, you find mental pictures. Sometimes you find them, too, on the front page of the second section.

For example, here is how a writer approached a story about Konica film, which was about to compete with Kodak and Fuji in the American market:

> Next to Eastman Kodak Co.'s yellow boxes
> and Fuji Film Co.'s green boxes will soon
> appear bright blue boxes of Konica film.

Immediately I see those colorful stacks of film boxes behind the cash register at the drugstore, and I read on into what could have been a dreary subject indeed. The story was saved by a writer doing her job back on page 33 to make the lead work.

I know I've devoted a lot of space to introductory sentences—more, as you'll soon see, than I devote to the writing of the whole piece. But the lead is so critically important. If you can figure out how to get your reader over the interest deadline, though, you're ready for the next step, where your skill will be tested again to keep the reader you have won.

Stray Notes

You have to feel pity for the poor copy editor who
spends his career removing adverbs from the middle
of infinitives, serene in his faith that these acts of piety
will assure him a place in blue-pencil heaven. Often,
in fact, what he has done is soil the copy, not clean
it up.

Consider this, from the *Washington Times:*

> A federal judge yesterday delayed . . . his
> order forcing an 800-inmate reduction in
> the D.C. jail population after the city
> agreed *gradually to lower* the jail count.

Of course, we don't know who the culprit is here;
it may have been the writer or the copy editor who
took *gradually* out of its proper place and exposed
the sentence to ambiguity.

Left to split the infinitive (*to gradually lower*),
gradually tells us that the city will reduce its jail population gradually. When the abverb is moved forward,

it could make the sentence mean that the city gradually agreed—that is, the city agreed bit by bit.

It is a myth that infinitives are sacred and should never be split. If splitting an infinitive gets the precise meaning you want, split it in good conscience. But to needlessly split an infinitive (as I have just done) is vandalism. Sometimes your sentence will be unaffected by splitting or not splitting. Then you have to let your ear tell you what to do.

From the *Boston Herald:*

> Four others were taken into custody when
> they arrived at the apartment to allegedly
> buy drugs, B—— said.

My ear wouldn't have heard it that way.

13

===

WRITING AS THE CROW FLIES

=

Stick with your outline, from A to B to C, and never double back. Why you need transitions.

An ugly streak of the pedagog in me says that, before we get to the actual writing process, I should recap all the brilliant points I made in the last two chapters, but I'll spare you that. It's enough to say that at this point you have produced a nutshell summary of the theme or thrust of your piece; have listed in proper order the major topics you will have to cover to support the summary; and have fashioned an introduction guaranteed to lure the reader into your masterwork.

To put it another way, you have decided where you are going (the nutshell summary), what direction to start in (the lead), and the major landmarks you will pass on the way (the topic list). Now all you have to do is follow that map.

I won't say the rest is child's play, but writing the story will be much easier now that you have mapped your course. Now you are free of worry about so many things that block a writer, such as wondering where you're going next with the thing. As for your creative genius (which we all know we have within us if only editors would give it a chance): Was it stifled while you plodded through those mechanical preparations? Well, now you can let your illumined being overrun the pages as, carefree, you write your way through the story.

First, obviously, you set down the lead you have shrewdly designed, now carved and polished to perfection. Next you transit to your nutshell summary, showing how the lead illustrates the broader subject, the main theme of your piece. (One writer I know calls this the "expander" section.)

Now to your road map, the list of topics you will have to cover to confirm the thesis of your nutshell summary. Here is Topic A with all of its subtopics: the list of facts and quotes that support Topic A. And here, collected in one stack, is the material that supports every item on your list. Put everything else out of your mind now and write Topic A. Complete A and dispose of it, once and for all.

Some writers fear that if they do a thorough job on Topic A the reader will become bored. So they hit it a lick or two and move on to Topic B, intending to sneak in the remaining Topic A material later on. Do not be tempted. That is a sure way to destroy the structure of the story, and if a story loses its structure, it most certainly will lose its readers. They will not put up with meandering from C back to A, on to D, and back to B. In following a road map you would not pass the second landmark, then double back to the first again.

I once knew a writer who wrote in ever expanding circles. The first time around, he used his nutshell summary. Then, in a widening circle, he would touch every topic again, expanding each slightly. Then he would go around again, covering the same topics more thoroughly, and so on. It was a dizzying thing to read —and hell to edit. But even that is preferable to bouncing back and forth among the topics with no apparent pattern.

So I repeat, complete Topic A and dispose of it once and for all before you turn to Topic B. If you fear Topic A is running too long, cut something out. Rewrite the A section to squeeze it down to digestible size.

Then it's on to Topic B—and it's crisis time again. If you do not make a sure transition from A to B, the reader may get lost. Unaware that you shifted the topic of conversation, as it were, he may stumble as he tries to fit this new information into the context of the old. In an ideal transition, Topic A ends with some statement or fact that can be picked up at the start of B and veered into the new topic. That kind of transition is so smooth that the reader moves with the writer effortlessly into the new material. He doesn't even know he has been manipulated.

For example: At one point in *A Stillness at Appomattox*, Bruce Catton is finishing a section in which he describes in detail the low morale in the ranks after a deadly siege of trench warfare. Next he wants to discuss the weaknesses among the Union generals, the failures of this one and that, the good points of others. He eases from the enlisted men's morale to the character of the generals in stages:

> One of his colonels wrote that he had had neither an unbroken night's sleep nor a change of clothing since May 5, and another remarked that he was so groggy with fatigue that it was impossible for him to write an intelligent letter to his family.

Now a half step:

> And General Warren, sensitive and high-strung, turned to another officer and burst out: "For 30 days it has been one funeral procession past me, and it is too much."

To full transition:

> Warren was showing the strain, and both Grant and Meade were noticing it. He had been a good friend of Meade.

And on Catton goes, into the merits and weaknesses of the various generals at this stage of the war, while the readers follow with no sense of hitting a bump.

The Warren quote was appropriate in the morale section and provided a hinge to turn the reader into the next subject.

That may seem like an extraordinary stroke of luck, that Warren quote. But if you really look for transitional devices, they can be found. True, the smooth transition requires the writer to do some work, but it can be achieved.

The writer isn't doing *any* work when he tries to transit by writing *meanwhile* or *meantime*. Many lazy writers try to get away with that, often forgetting that both words mean *at the same time*. Occasionally *meanwhile* is accurately used, but often it is not. Either way, it's a transitional device best left to the old Saturday-afternoon Western movies, as in *Meanwhile, back at the ranch . . .*

Another transitional failure is what has been called the "not-goldfish-but" device. The name comes from the attempt by a columnist to move from an item about goldfish to the next, unrelated item. I grant that this technique can be applied universally and requires no effort by the writer, but the result is obviously absurd.

Still another way to transit—or, more accurately, to avoid hard work while trying to transit—is the typographical device. Sometimes it's necessary in a very long piece, but it can be bumpy, as I am about to demonstrate here.

* * *

A frequent threat to the unity of a story is a fact or anecdote that is only vaguely related to the main theme. It doesn't really fit into any of the topics in the outline, and yet it is so interesting that the writer feels he simply must work it in somehow. So he takes a sledgehammer and drives it into the trunk of the story, splitting the unity and breaking the reader's train of thought. I urge you—no matter how enamored you are of this extraneous fact—do not force it into the story. Better to forget it. But if that brings tears to your eyes, you might offer it as a short companion piece. Otherwise, be ruthless.

So now you have written your way through all the major topics on your list, slipping in quotes and bits of descriptive color from your parallel list, and it's time to conclude the piece. Now you transit into the special ending you reserved back when you first combed through your material after all the research was done. You'll be glad now that you reserved it; you've saved yourself the agony of trying desperately to find a way to end the thing and go to bed.

Tack it on, and there you are: a beautiful piece of writing, set down in an orderly way, full of color and action—impossible to put down, as the book reviewers say. Congratulations.

Stray Notes

Alarms should ring when you find you have committed two or more *after*s in the same sentence.

This, from the *Chicago Tribune*, isn't impossible to read, but it spins my head at first:

> After the Lions released Thomas when
> holdout Eddie Murray returned, Ditka
> re-signed the veteran after Bears' kicker
> John Roveto slumped.

With the *when* in there, this sentence becomes a three-cushion shot, requiring an instant replay.

A second *after* doesn't necessarily ruin a sentence, but it should warn the writer to stop and check.

THE REMUNERATION OF PECCANCY

. . . is death, of course. And if you "write" that way, with ponderous prose, you're dead as a writer.

Lined up at the rail of the troopship St. Mihiel on a February morning in 1943, we got our first glimpse of an Aleutian Island. It just lay there in the rain, gray and barren—not a tree or even a shrub in sight. The man next to me studied the scene for a while, then spoke:

> There must be some force which militates against the germination of vegetation.

Trees can't grow in the miserable climate of the Aleutian Islands, but my comrade-in-arms just couldn't bring himself to put it that simply. He was a pompous man, and everything he said had to be pompous; hence, *militates against the germination of vegetation.*

That night I wrote down his comment and swore that as long as I lived, I would never, never talk or write that way. I further swore a knightly oath that wherever I encountered that kind of ponderous writing, I would try to stamp it out.

Thus, in my reading of the *Detroit News* I have kept an eye out for these offenses. Here are some I clipped out:

> Meanwhile, Democratic senators were
> unsuccessful in passing of their version of
> a jobs bill.

Why not simply *failed to pass their version?* That's the plain way to say it. The ponderous language only clogs up the sentence and makes it harder to read.

> The sophisticated plant will provide
> phosphorus removal to prevent excessive
> algae.

That's just a bloated way of saying, *The sophisticated plant will remove phosphorus*, so why not say it that way instead of *providing phosphorus removal?*

> By living outside the Detroit school
> district, Mrs. M—— was in violation of
> state law.

The same offense, committed by the *Washington Post:*

> The suit . . . contends that the dismissals
> were in violation of patient care standards.

Why have people be *in violation of* law when just plain *violated* would do?

From the *Baltimore Sun:*

> However, there has not been a cancellation
> of the season.

Better: *However, the season has not been canceled.*

The *Detroit News:*

> The implant operation took place early
> yesterday.

Beware of things that *take place.* Usually there's a direct, active way to say these things. In this example the writer could have said, *Surgeons implanted the heart early yesterday.* (And since the writer did not say that, an editor might have seen to it.)

From the *Detroit News:*

> He said arraignments in the case will be
> held next week.

Events that are *held* are like events that *take place:* They often involve an abstract noun. A more direct way to say that is, *He said the defendants would be arraigned next week.*

The *Chicago Tribune:*

> Doctors and others worked for more than
> two hours in a resuscitation attempt.

Back to the *Detroit News:*

> The outbreak of hostilities came in 1882
> when Jonse Hatfield ran away with Rose
> Ann McCoy.

Better to write: *Hostilities broke out in . . .*

> Recommendations of a company are
> expected by the council from Mayor
> Coleman A. Young in late May.

What kind of writing is this? The writer went out
of his way to make it not only nouny but passive
too. Try this instead: *The council expects Mayor
Coleman A. Young to recommend a company in late
May.*

City hall reporters write that way elsewhere too, as
this specimen from the *New York Daily News* shows:

> Announcement of the auction was made by
> Mayor Koch at City Hall.

To make my point clear, let me line up a few of these examples alongside the direct, natural way to say them:

... worked for more than two hours *in a resuscitation attempt.*	... tried for more than two hours *to resuscitate* him.
Arraignments will be held next week.	Defendants will be *arraigned* next week.
She was *in violation of* ...	She *violated* ...
... *implant operation* took place.	Surgeons *implanted* the heart.
Recommendations of a company are expected by the council from the mayor.	The council expects the mayor to *recommend* a company.

The crime that all these examples have in common is this: Each writer avoided direct language by changing the verb into a noun. *Arraigned* became *arraignments,* and the verb became the weak *will be held.* *Implanted* became *implant operation,* so to get a verb back into the sentence, *took place* had to be supplied. The writer transformed *recommend* into *recommendations* and then had to squirt in a heavy dose of prepositions to work out the sentence: *Recommendations of a company are expected* by *the council* from *the mayor.* A woman who simply *violated* the law was put in *violation* of the law, requiring two prepositions.

Let's deal with those prepositions first. They come close to the sin of "compound prepositions," of which Fowler wrote: "They are almost the worst element in modern English, stuffing up the newspaper columns with a compost of nouny abstractions." But multiple prepositions, which serve to obstruct a sentence rather then move it forward, are what you get when you insist on turning decent verbs into abstract nouns.

What you also get is what Wilson Follett decries as noun-plague. Fowler discusses the problem, too, under the heading *-tion and other -ion endings:* Let's hear Fowler first:

> Turgid flabby English . . . is full of abstract nouns; the commonest ending of abstract nouns is "*-tion*"; and to count the "*-ion*" words in what one has written, or, better, to cultivate an ear that without special orders challenges them as they come, is one of the simplest and most effective means of making oneself less unreadable. . . . Some nouny writers . . . so stud their sentences with *-tions* that the mere sound becomes an offense.

An example from the *St. Louis Post-Dispatch:*

> Information concerning a free-for-all involving as many as 40 people on the

Current River over the Labor Day weekend
will go to a U. S. Attorney this week for a
decision on possible prosecution.

And now, Follett, denouncing a style that

tends to turn thought into a chain of static
abstractions linked by prepositions and by
weak verbs generally in the passive voice.
... Many abstract nouns in English end
in *-tion*, and the effect on the ear of
stringing several of them together is
narcotic.

Anyone with a short attention span may stop reading right here. If you write with verbs instead of
transforming them into nouns and you rid sentences
of *-ion* words (and some *-ing* words) wherever possible, you will improve your writing and editing skills
immensely.

There is more, however, that you can do, for these
specific sins are only part of the broader offense we
set out to discuss, called jargon by some, periphrasis
by others; I call it pomposity. Some writers abhor the
forthright statement, preferring to coat it with noble
language that carries the weight of their importance
(or, perhaps, the weight of their insecurity).

The jargoneer, says Sir Arthur Quiller-Couch,
would have written, "Render unto Caesar the things
that appertain to that potentate." And it was a jargoneer, he says, who wrote, "He was conveyed to his

place of residence in an intoxicated condition," when what he really meant was, "He was carried home drunk."

Fowler, who calls this periphrasis, has this to say:

> These good people feel that there is an almost indecent nakedness, a reversion to barbarism, in saying, "No news is good news," instead of, "The absence of intelligence is an indication of satisfactory developments."

It is a form of periphrasis to say that so-and-so *resides on the city's east side* instead of letting him live there; to persist in calling all lawyers *attorneys;* and to automatically substitute *litany* for *list* every time the word appears.

It is also a form of periphrasis—or jargon, as Quiller-Couch prefers—to use such expressions as *in regard to, with respect to, as to whether, in this case, in this instance, associated with, in the neighborhood of, in terms of*—to name a few

An example from the *St. Louis Post-Dispatch:*

> . . . a short time before parents picked up their children, who *in most cases* were left in B——'s care all day.

Strike *in most cases* and substitute *usually*.

Here's one of my favorites, one I've cited many times over the years. It's from the *New York Times:*

> But *in the case of* Representative James
> Armstrong Mackay of Atlanta this was
> *not altogether the case.*

From the opening paragraph of a story in *Architectural Digest:*

> When an architect dies, *it is often the case*
> *that* he leaves behind a number. . . *It is*
> *often the case, as well, that* these
> projects . . .

Without any loss of meaning, this can be simplified to: *When an architect dies, often he leaves behind a number. . . Often, too, these projects . . .*

Fowler says this about the word *case:*

> There is perhaps no single word so freely
> resorted to as a trouble-saver, and
> consequently responsible for so much
> flabby writing.

Basis often invites similar wordiness, as shown by this from the *Denver Post:*

> There are also are [*sic*] immediate deals at
> Loveland and Keystone, the only resorts
> now open on a daily basis.

Why not just *the only resorts now open daily?*

Now, please don't tell me that you work on a news-paper and don't have time to work on these kinds of things to improve your writing. If you can't do it now, while you're writing, when will you do it? When you retire? (It's like saying, "We don't have time for peace talks now; we're busy fighting a war.") To say you don't have time to do it now is to say that a year from now—20 years from now—you don't expect to be a better writer than you are today. You won't be, either. And I'll guarantee that if you spend a few years writing slovenly prose, you'll never recover from it. As a writer, you are dead.

Stray Notes

To find one of these would be an oddity—or so I thought. To find two is bizarre. But here they are, by different writers, appearing only six days apart in the *Detroit News:*

> McGeorge Bundy . . . told the association that diffusing the population bomb . . .

> "My job is to diffuse the situation," he says.

Then I found this in the *Washington Post:*

> They called the police, who diffused a bomb that . . .

What ever happened to *defuse?*

INFRASTRUCTURE ON THE RIVER KWAI

Why, if we all denounce clichés, do writers keep on using them? How to keep your guard up.

Although unconfirmed at the time, the first reported sighting of a parameter west of the Mississippi came in 1969, a sinister sign that the word had escaped from Eastern intellectual circles and was loose in the land. Now we may never see the end of it.

A lawn enthusiast in, say, Cleveland measures the length and width of his yard, calculates the high cost of fertilizer, and concludes, *Well, at least I know the parameters of the problem.* A new middle-management executive in Connecticut is briefed on his duties and reports that he *quickly learned the parameters of his authority.* And one reads in the *Detroit News* that a music group called The Dead Kennedys *fit into the "hardcore" parameters perfectly.*

The word is everywhere, and I would wager that few of its users know what it means. If they looked it up in a dictionary, they would find a baffling definition, understandable only to mathematicians, its rightful owners.

Etymological sleuths may never discover how the

word first got away from mathematicians and into the general population, but I suspect the sociologists in this. One of them, my theory goes, overheard a mathematician say *parameter* in some interdisciplinary gathering and seized upon it as a simply marvelous new word with roughly the same meaning as *perimeter*—but not so, uh, ordinary. This carrier casually slipped the word into a conversation with his own colleagues, and from there it spread into the lexicon of the humanities. No doubt some of the junk dictionaries will soon list a secondary meaning of *parameter: 2. boundary; same as perimeter.* (One may already have done it while my back was turned.)

Well, I have disported too long about *parameter,* but I thought my fanciful history of the development of the word was a good way to get into the matter of fad words—or vogue words, as both Fowler and Follett call them—which often turn into the most sickening of clichés.

No writer needs to be told that clichés are bad. Yet by some insidious means, they keep showing up in print. It's as if every publication has a secret agent who waits until everything is written and everybody has gone home and then stealthily substitutes *litany* for *list* every time he finds the word.

How did *litany* become a synonym for *list?* (It isn't really.) The record is not yet clear, but I suspect it developed in about the same way *parameter* did in my version above. Somebody used *litany* in a borderline way that caused a listener or reader to think it was a hot-damn new word for *list*. He didn't bother to look it up and couldn't wait to jam it into a story or conversation, right or wrong. Then it spread quickly from one novelty seeker to another until, in some shops, a writer who still uses *list* instead of *litany* is considered stodgy. Just doesn't know how to *hype* his copy, to use another nauseating word of the hour.

Take *infrastructure*. We began to hear a lot about infrastructures during the Vietnam War, when we were regularly assured that the Viet Cong infrastructure was either severely damaged or still intact. The word was not in contemporary dictionaries, so you had to combine the meanings of *infra* and *structure* to deduce what the war correspondents were writing about. (From the usual context, though, it seemed to mean *command* or *governmental structure*.) Now *infrastructure* appears in dictionaries and, mercilessly, in our newspapers. It seems that we need billions of dollars (usually *in public funding*) to rebuild our bridges and highways, but a newspaper reporter today is pleased to write *infrastructure* because that is the vogue.

Actually, *infrastructure* is a fairly precise—if ugly—word, although it means much more than bridges and roads. But many of these trite expressions are far off the mark, or, from overuse, their original meanings have been forgotten. This can lead a writer to try to fortify the word or term, often with idiotic results.

Thus, on a Washington, D.C., radio commercial you can hear a store advertise that it has *plenty of ample parking*.

Similar things happened when a great vogue swept through the sports fraternity, particularly broadcast sports, a few years ago. Athletes were no longer fast or quick. They had *great speed* or *great quickness*. (A football coach in Detroit was quoted in the *News* as saying that one of his backs had *good awareness*.) Repeated over and over, these clichés lost their punch and their meaning. When a running back was tackled from behind, a network radio commentator (a former coach) explained that the back *didn't have enough great speed*. And on network television a football analyst said of a player, *He's got great speed—not super-duper speed, but great speed*.

The current expression *I can live with it* offers an extreme example of how a hackneyed phrase, repeated millions of times, loses its meaning. In San Angelo, Texas, a judge sentenced a killer to death (to *die by lethal injection*, the *Detroit News* reported). The killer's response to the death sentence: "I can live with it."

All right, we have reached the point in this little essay where you may wonder where it is going. Is this about clichés or about vogue words? It is about both, because I think many clichés result from the eagerness of writers to leap onto the hottest new word or phrase, thus quickly turning them into clichés.

Why, if we all denounce clichés, do we keep on using them? My theory is that we have been inadequately warned about clichés. Usually a warning is delivered with a list of clichés to avoid. The young writer looks them over, agrees they are bad, and resolves never to use any of them, as if he had just read the complete and final list of clichés—next lesson, please. He remembers those (perhaps), but he is not on guard against "new" ones.

The first time a crime reporter wrote that so-and-so shot his wife and then *turned the gun on himself*, it must have seemed like a fresh way to describe an all-too-common event. Today, though, many writers feel compelled to use this cliché again and again, as if federal law requires it. A *Washington Post* account of a domestic tragedy managed to use the phrase twice in the same four-paragraph story, thus earning double credit in the *Great Book of Clichés*.

Even Joyce Carol Oates wrote, in her fascinating novel *them:*

> A woman tried to kill him, firing two shots
> into his chest and then turning the gun on
> herself.

The cliché factory works around the clock. A writer with any pride—and there are no *real* writers without it—will brace himself constantly against some other writer's trick phrase or odd use of a familiar word. A phrase that a writer admires may, indeed, be worthy, but he must resist the temptation to adopt it as his own, first because it would be shameless theft, and second because a thousand other imitative writers are sure to do the same. That is the way to avoid clichés. And the writer who shuns the fashionable will always be in style.

Stray Notes

From the *New York Times:*

> The defense has argued that Mr. S—— was
> drunk and died as a result of injuries
> sustained during his frenzied struggle.

To sustain means *to endure, to withstand.* If the man
died of his injuries, he did not sustain them.

From a Book-of-the-Month Club brochure:

> No matter how familiar you are with the
> Civil War and its leading protagonists,
> you'll find this book irresistible.

From the *Detroit News:*

> But though the primary protagonists here
> are . . .

There can be only one protagonist, because the
word means *first actor.* To say *primary first actor* is
redundant: a *first first actor.*

That reminds me of the advertising campaign describing the *Wall Street Journal* as "the daily diary of the American dream." What do you suppose those ad men think *diary* means?

16

=

STAYING
OUT OF
MACY'S
WINDOW

=

Dangling modifiers can produce ludicrous results, and you may find yourself on public display.

This subject is going to be unpleasant, to me and to you. We've been lectured numb about it all through school and intermittently since; who wants to return to it again?

But return we must. Evidence abounds that the subject needs to be revisited, and unless it is, you may find yourself on display in *The New Yorker*, as the *Nashua* (N.H.) *Telegraph* did recently:

> Although only two months old, Arcaro
> said the system is "still a white elephant"
> and insisted the city "wind down" the
> experiment.

The New Yorker's comment: "Talkative little fellow, that Arcaro."

Laughter all around, except in Nashua. It's easy to laugh when others make this mistake. And we hoot at ludicrous examples cited in reference books, like this one from Strunk and White:

> Being in a dilapidated condition, I was able
> to buy the house very cheap.

Or this from Follett:

> Sitting on the porch last night, a comet and
> five shooting stars were seen.

The problem, of course, is the "dangling modifier," as some call it, or just plain "dangler," as Follett prefers. Simply put, the rule is that the modifying word or phrase applies to the subject immediately following.

In the Nashua example, obviously, it was not Arcaro who was two months old, although Arcaro immediately followed the modifier. The writer should have sensed that something was amiss. The sentence should have read:

> Although only two months old, the system
> is "still a white elephant," Arcaro said. . . .

But why look for examples in New Hampshire? Here's one from the *Detroit News:*

> When watching her perform, she displays
> the style, grace and technique that seem to
> put her in the same class as Retton and
> McNamara.

Most of you will spot the mistake immediately. The dangler here is the modifying phrase *When watching her perform.* The phrase must apply to what immediately follows (the subject of the sentence)—here, the pronoun *she*. But it cannot apply. *She* is not watching her perform; some unidentified person (the writer, no doubt) is watching her. So the modifier is not properly attached.

How to correct the sentence? It happens that the best way is simply to knock out the modifying phrase altogether. It makes no sense. Just start the sentence with *She*. But if you *had* to make a sentence out of all the elements of the original, it could read:

> When others are watching her perform,
> she displays the style, grace . . .

But the sentence remains illogical. If no one is watching her perform, how can she display anything? From *USA Today:*

> But realizing the seriousness of drug abuse
> and the vastly differing views on how to
> cope with the problem, it was stricken
> from the agenda.

The sentence doesn't say who did all that realizing, unless *it* did it, as the construction of that sentence would have us believe. The first 19 words constitute a dangling modifier.

Also from *USA Today:*

> Because he can bench press 420 pounds and
> squat 600, Emrich thinks Perry's strength
> could be the best among the Bears.

For all we know, this fellow Emrich, a member of the Chicago Bears' coaching staff, may be able to perform those feats of strength, as this sentence—so constructed—tells us. Even so, I'd bet my woodpile that the writer meant that Perry the player, not Emrich the coach, lifts those weights. That could have been said accurately in this way:

> Because he can bench press 420 pounds and squat 600, Perry's strength could be the best among the Bears, Emrich thinks.

Here's another example, from the *Detroit News:*

> The future status of the tunnel itself is in doubt. When opened in 1930, the operators were given a 60-year franchise.

The dangler here is *When opened in 1930.* What it applies to, as written, is the subject of the main verb, *the operators.* But it's the tunnel that was opened in 1930, not the operators, as the sentence says. It could be corrected to read:

> When it opened in 1930, the operators were given . . .

(The antecedent for *it* is *tunnel* in the preceding sentence.)

Another from the *Detroit News:*

> Initially ruled a suicide, a six-member
> Livingston County jury later decided that
> W—— was murdered.

Common sense tells the reader that it was not the jury that was ruled a suicide, but the sentence says it was. This one, though, is not so easily corrected, unless the writer is willing to accept the passive voice:

> Initially ruled a suicide, W——'s death was
> later classified as murder by a six-member
> Livingston County jury.

It's not great prose, but at least the modifying clause, *Initially ruled a suicide*, has been attached where it belongs: to W——'s death. Better to write:

> W——'s death was initially ruled a suicide,
> but a six-member Livingston County jury
> later classified it as murder.

Another example:

> Complaining that department budgets have
> already been slashed "to the bone," the
> latest cutback order left many county
> officials wondering aloud where they'll find
> another 20 percent to snip.

The sentence would have us believe that *the latest cutback order* contains a complaint that department budgets have already been slashed to the bone. I'm sure that's not what the writer meant. What he meant was:

> Complaining that department budgets have already been slashed "to the bone," county officials wondered aloud where they would find another . . .

Here are a couple that are similarly illogical but easily corrected:

> After robbing the four, witnesses said
> R—— used his pistol to sexually assault the woman clerk.

> After being tied up in the rear of his truck, police said the Bell worker managed to escape unhurt.

The second one says it was the police who were tied up in the rear of the truck, because the modifying phrase attaches directly to *police*. The sentence could be improved simply by inserting a comma after *police said*, but a better way would be to move *police said* to the end of the sentence so that it doesn't intervene between the modifier and the noun it modifies.

The same goes for the first example. Put a comma after *witnesses said*, or move the attribution to the end of the sentence, out of harm's way. (I'm not even going to comment on the peculiar wording of the rest of that sentence.)

One more:

> After six months in office, a majority of
> Michigan residents disapprove of the way
> Blanchard is handling his job.

Surely everybody recognizes the fault by now. The modifier, *After six months in office*, should be attached directly to *Blanchard*, not to *a majority of Michigan residents*.

This is the way to test yourself if you have trouble with danglers: When you start a sentence with a modifying phrase like *Sitting on the porch last night*, make sure that the subject it modifies follows immediately. If what follows immediately is *a comet and five shooting stars*, it should dawn on you quickly that a comet and five shooting stars were not sitting on the porch last night. Therefore, the modifier is not properly attached.

What causes the mistake? Some writers lack logical minds and simply fail to see how illogical these sentences are. Some libertarians may believe that if the reader can surmise the meaning, that's good enough (it never is). And some good writers occasionally lapse; their minds wander while they're writing or revising, and they forget how they started the sentence. In those moments, they should be able to rely on their editors, but editors' minds have been known to wander too.

If you and your editor lapse in synchrony, and if your mistake turns out to be funny, you may find yourself naked in Macy's window.

Afterthought: In this example from the *Denver Post*, the modifying clause doesn't dangle, but it certainly helps destroy the sentence:

> Sponsored by Foods and Wines from France, the promotion and information center for imported French wine and food specialties under the direction of the International Association of the Maitres-Conseils in French Gastronomy, the competition's semifinals were held in 14 U.S. cities.

The perpetrator of that sentence should be put on modifier probation, forbidden to open *any* sentence with a modifying clause—dangling or otherwise—for at least one year.

Stray Notes

I'm not going to carry on about it, but a quick word about pronouns seems to be in order.

Look at this, from the *Miami Herald:*

> The west end looked as if they had been
> attacked by bomb-laden anti-beach house
> terrorists, not a natural force.

The previous sentence had told how 600 homes had been damaged or destroyed in the storm, so evidently the writer thought those homes could serve as the antecedent for *they* in the next sentence. That might have worked if there had been no intervening noun, but there was: *the west end.* So the sentence should read, *The west end looked as if it had been . . .*

The next example, from the *Detroit News,* shows the deep trouble that leapfrogging pronouns can get you into:

> Key members of the administration are
> with the president during a five-day
> vacation at his nearby ranch. They believe
> he will die within six months.

That was printed long before President Reagan had surgery, so the evident meaning was doubly shocking. What else could it possibly mean? Nothing else, unless you look back to the previous paragraph, which describes the failing health of Konstantin Chernenko, then the Soviet leader. But two sentences later, the writer cannot hope to claim any antecedent for the pronoun *he* other than *the president.*

17

ADVERBS
AMUCK

Unless you're doing Tom Swifties, an overdose of adverbs can eat holes in a piece of writing.

Twenty-odd years ago, a joke form called Tom Swifties swept across the country, temporarily displacing Knock Knock as the favorite sally for those who like their humor well planned. The technique of Tom Swifties was to attribute a quote to somebody and add an adverb that produced a play on words. It added to the merriment, of course, if the quote itself was appropriate. For example:

> "I see nothing wrong with ambition," said
> the bishop archly.

But for many practitioners, there was fun enough just in the attribution:

> . . . ," said Mother earthily.
> . . . ," said Jack frostily.

Those may be feeble examples, but they're the best I can do on the spur of the moment. I can't remember any of the real specimens from that period, except the one that gave the joke form its name:

. . . ," said Tom swiftly.

Tom Swiftly . . . Tom Swift . . . Tom Swifties. Get it? No? Then you also need to know that early in the century a series of boys' books by Victor Appleton featured as their hero young Tom Swift, whose adventures bore such titles as *Tom Swift and His Electric Runabout* and *Tom Swift and His Airship*. Appleton often referred to Tom as "the lad" and had his characters exclaim things like "Bless my collar button!" But the books are best remembered for Appleton's adverbs. It was hard for an Appleton character to say anything without an adverb: "remarked Mr. Swift musingly"; "asked Mr. Swift anxiously"; "responded Tom calmly." Hence the adverbial humor of Tom Swifties.

These jokes had the decency to fade from popularity before they became too nauseating (unlike the Good News–Bad News jokes of yesterday, today, and apparently forever). For a while—say, about six days —Tom Swifties were fun, and they did serve to remind us that adverbs can eat holes in a piece of writing and expose the author to public ridicule.

I regale you with all this because I often find needless or peculiar adverbs in my reading, as exemplified by this, from an otherwise commendable *Detroit News* story:

> "I am going to go out on a limb with this prediction," John T——, director of the state campaign finance reporting, said cynically.

And with that, Mr. T—— predicted something perfectly safe and obvious.

Why *cynically?* The adverb stopped me right there in the middle of the story. There was nothing cynical about what he said, as far as I could see, unless I misunderstood the meaning of the word. But a dictionary check confirmed that *cynical* meant "a contemptuous disbelief in human goodness and sincerity." So *cynically* was not the adverb the writer wanted. How, then, did Mr. T—— say what he said? What was the right adverb?

(Notice, now, that I am no longer reading the story; instead, I am mumbling to myself and thumbing through a dictionary. By dropping in that adverb, the writer has diverted my attention, and he may never get me back.)

Sardonically, perhaps? Back to the dictionary. "Disdainfully or bitterly sneering, ironical, or sarcastic." No, Mr. T—— didn't seem to be doing that. "See *sarcastic,*" the dictionary advised, so I tried that. But there was nothing taunting, sneering, cutting, or caustic about what Mr. T—— said.

Well, enough of my quest. I finally concluded that Mr. T—— was just trying to be funny, so the writer might have used the adverb *jocosely* or even *jocularly*. Even so, the reader's attention would have focused on the sore-thumb adverb instead of the sense of the story, so the writer would have lost him anyway, at least for a moment. Besides, if Mr. T——'s humor is indeed humor, the reader should be able to get it without printed instructions.

(At one point in this dictionary search, my eye fell on *sans-culottic*, and I spent some more time trying to imagine a circumstance in which a character in a story might say something *sans-culotically*. That really diverted my attention.)

I was distracted, too, by an adverb high up in a *Washington Post* story that reported *the broadcast has been exemplarily written*. And then the adverbs began to pile up: *ludicrously charged, off-puttingly austere, rabidly maligned, compatibly back-to-back*. They stood out on the page as if printed in boldface.

Let me turn to another author (to be nameless here), one who made his reputation with his first novel, about the sordid inner workings of politics in Washington, D.C. The book became a movie, and although I can't recall how well it did west of the Potomac, it drew big crowds in Washington.

I must concede, the author wrote a gripping story, but as I got into the book, I became increasingly aware of the adverbs. They never ceased. This man was worse than Victor Appleton. So it got to be a parlor trick at my house while the book was in vogue. When we had guests, I would try to steer the conversation to this book, if it didn't come up naturally, and then I would proclaim that the author was the worst adverb abuser I had ever encountered. With that, I would put on my show. I would let the book fall open at random or ask a guest to pick a page, any page. And then I would read aloud from the dialog that appeared there.

I'll do the same thing right now, and I'll take a blood oath that my page selection is entirely random. The book falls open to pages 204 and 205, and I read:

> . . . ," the nominee said quietly.
> . . . ," Arly Richardson said slowly.
> . . . ," the nominee said pleasantly.
> . . . ," he said pleasantly.
> . . . ," Senator Danta said quietly.
> . . . ," Hal Fry said softly.
> . . . ," Hal Fry said bitterly.
> . . . ," K. K. said, more lightly.

You think that was an accident? Well, let's cut the deck again and see what we find (it opens to 344–345):

> . . . ," Brigham Anderson said rather sharply.
> . . . ," Lafe said humorously.
> . . . ," Brig said pleasantly.
> . . . ," he said lightly.
> . . . ," Senator Smith said, rather glumly.
> . . . ," Lafe said quickly.

Somewhere in the book there may be a page or two of dialog without adverbs, but not many. Believe me, this trick will stand up. If you doubt it, I'll confide the name of the book to you and you can try it yourself. You'll find *-ly* adverbs dropping on your head until you go mad.

The moral I hope you do *not* draw from this is that if you write a novel and pack in adverbs with every bit of dialog, you will have a best-seller and a million-dollar movie sale. This book succeeded because the author is a gifted storyteller, not because he is a great writer. Yet what I remember about the book, after all these years, is not the story but the adverbs.

Are adverbs necessary? Of course. It would be ridiculous to suggest that you should never use an adverb. The action you describe or the words you quote may not connote the full meaning, and you may have to spend an adverb to get it across. So do it. But be sure it is necessary and unobtrusive, which is hard to do if you insist on using *-ly* adverbs in attribution.

(Keep an ear out, too, for the dissonance of piled-on *-ly* words, as in this example from the *Los Angeles Times: Nearby, the old Union Church stands similarly ghostly.*)

If you doubt that one can write well with rationed adverbs, take a look at the dialog in a book I have praised before, Russell Baker's *Growing Up*. You won't find people saying things calmly, quietly, musingly, pleasantly, slowly, or bitterly on Baker's pages.

Finally, let me wheel out Wilson Follett again:

> Consciously or not, -*ly* is sensed as
> enfeebling to prose; it contributes to the
> sinuosities of style, but enervates its muscle.
> . . . With the rough justice of
> oversimplification it is often decreed that
> the fewer adverbs writing can get along
> with, the better it is.

You might infer that Follett thinks the decree is a bit too harsh, and it may be. But if it forces the writer to seek the precise noun and the precise verb that will eliminate the need for an adverb, then I'm all for the rough justice of oversimplification. Better that than to let adverbs run amuck.

Stray Notes

—

Both of these are from the *Detroit News:*

> A baby boy abandoned hours after his birth
> in a garbage dumpster is now 2 months old
> and the "smilingest child you'd ever hope
> to see."

A damned unpleasant accouchement for Mom,
though.

How about *abandoned in a garbage dumpster hours
after his birth?*

> A Southfield man has been charged with a
> second murder of a Detroit go-go dancer.

And they say you only live once.

Better to write *charged with the murder of a second
Detroit go-go dancer.*

STYLE
AND
NO STYLE

===

A writer's passion to develop a distinctive style may lead him into a morass. A fool and his thesaurus.

How many times have you heard other writers say it, or said it yourself: I'm trying to develop an individual style, a distinctive way of writing that's my own, not like any other writer's.

I've heard it most of my life, sometimes out of my own mouth. Nothing wrong with it, necessarily. It may even be a healthy sign that the writer is not just running off at the typewriter, accepting any words that happen to appear on the paper in whatever form. At least the writer knows that to learn to write well he will have to sweat and swear and rewrite and rewrite again. That's a start.

But what a shame that the writer may suffer through all that torment only to make matters worse. For if the passion to be unique is misguided, if it overwhelms the passion to write well, the writer could be headed down a trail overgrown with poison polysyllables and stylistic stunts—like the antic alliteration I have just written.

Tricks will not produce your distinctive style. Any

fool can turn to his thesaurus and find a combination of alliterative words or novelty words or long words to substitute for what he takes to be the commonplaces he has written.

I know a writer who struggled through what I called his Woolworth phase. During that period, you could see him at his desk, tracing down the pages of his thesaurus in search of a trinket word to replace anything that looked natural in his copy. He turned out miserable stuff. But the desire was there, and something (wise and patient editors, I'm sure) got him through that phase without permanent damage. Many never recover.

(Aside: I certainly do not condemn the thesaurus. It's invaluable when you can't recollect the precise word with just the nuance you want. The thesaurus may help you find it again. But beware of any other-world discoveries you make while you're in there, and always check your newfound word in a dictionary before you use it.)

In *Time* magazine's early days, its editors feared that a plain rewrite of last week's newspapers might attract little attention and few readers, so they sought a distinctive *Time* style. They got it by (among other things) piled-on adjectives—often preceding a person's name—and by a bizarre inversion of sentences.

As cited by Robert T. Elson in his friendly history, *TIME, INC.*, George Bernard Shaw was described as "mocking, mordant, misanthropic." The inverted sentences got as bad as this: "A ghastly ghoul prowled around a cemetery not far from Paris. Into family chapels went he, robbery of the dead intent upon."

Time's style was distinctive, all right, like the tattooed man in the carnival, and it prompted Wolcott Gibbs to do his classic parody in *The New Yorker*. "Backward ran sentences until reeled the mind," Gibbs wrote in the most-quoted line from that piece. "Where it will all end, knows God." But *Time* was doing some things right, of course, and as it matured it peeled off and discarded its freakish style.

The problem is not peculiar to journalism. Consider the reminiscences of W. Somerset Maugham, in a foreword written for the reprinting, many years later, of his incomparable novel *Of Human Bondage*. Maugham describes how, as a successful playwright, he retired from drama and turned again to the novel:

> For long after I became a writer by profession I spent much time on learning how to write and subjected myself to very tiresome training in the endeavour to improve my style. But these efforts I abandoned. . . . I no longer sought a jewelled prose and a rich texture. . . . I sought on the contrary plainness and simplicity. . . . I set out now with the notion of using only such [words] as were necessary to make my meaning clear.

And that brings us, finally, to the heart of this discourse: simplicity. Well, allow me two more words: precision and clarity, although in my mind they are all intertwined. If you can develop a style that meets these three tests, you are a writer.

Want another opinion? Here's the view of Dashiell Hammett, quoted in *Dashiell Hammett, A Life*, by Diane Johnson:

> . . . clarity is the first and greatest of literary
> virtues. The needlessly involved sentence,
> the clouded image, are not literary. They
> are anti-literary. . . . Simplicity and clarity
> . . . are the most elusive and difficult of
> literary accomplishments, and a high degree
> of skill is necessary to any writer who
> would win them.

And here are the Fowler brothers, H. W. and F. G., in *The King's English* (a good book to own, if you can find a copy):

> [The journalist] often thinks the length of
> his words and his capacity for dealing in
> the abstract to be signs of a superior mind.
> As long as that opinion prevails,
> improvement is out of the question. But if
> it could be established that simplicity was
> the true ideal, many more writers would be
> found capable of coming near it.

From the same source:

> Anyone who wishes to become a good
> writer should endeavour, before he allows
> himself to be tempted by the more showy
> qualities, to be direct, simple, brief,
> vigorous, and lucid.

Please permit me one more testimonial, this from
Herbert Read, praising Jonathan Swift in Read's book
English Prose Style:

> Swift's greatness consists in this fact, more
> than anything else, that however widely
> his vision might extend, however deep his
> insight, his mode of expression remained
> simple . . . and clearly comprehensible.

All right, I'm braced for it. You're about to complain that I began this little essay by discussing distinctive, individual styles and I seem to be winding it
down by preaching simplicity. But, you may ask, If
I write simply, how will I be different from other
writers who write simply?

Well, browse through some of the graceful essays
of E. B. White and you'll see. Try my favorite, "Farewell, My Lovely!" *There* is simplicity, and *there* is
the style of E. B. White, uniquely his own.

Your simple style will be unique if your personality
and your thought processes are unique—and of course

they are. The point is to let the reader see them. To develop your style, work not to hang ornaments on it but to strip away everything that is artificial, to scrape off the glaze so that your style becomes invisible. The reader then will not be distracted by your style; he will look right through it and see your wit, your emotions, your orderly mind—whatever you have going on inside. (If, of course, there is nothing going on in there, you're in deep trouble.) I'll even dare to suggest that the best style may be no style at all, but to achieve a perfect "no-style" requires a life sentence at hard labor.

Along the way, though, you will begin to get control of the thing, so that you can spurt a stream of words onto a hard news story or, by adjusting the nozzle, spray a gentle mist onto a feature. People will know who wrote it.

Stray Notes

Negatives often cause trouble, sometimes making the reader backtrack to make sure of the meaning, sometimes making the statement dead wrong. An example, from the *Wall Street Journal:*

> This thriving shop, named for its founder
> and Sam's father, *doesn't succeed* because
> Mr. Harris is a modern merchandising
> genius.

That sentence seems to tell us why the shop doesn't succeed, when, in fact, the shop does. The sense the writer wanted is that the shop succeeds, although Mr. Harris is not a modern merchandising genius.

And when the *Detroit News* reports that *all Germans were not responsible for the Nazi crimes*, the sentence seems to mean *no* Germans were responsible. With the misplaced *not* relocated, the sentence would read, correctly, that *not all Germans were responsible . . .*

ASIDE
TO
YOUNG
WRITERS

====

First learn how to cut loose (then how to rein in). Don't wait to be sent on a literary errand.

As that title states, this is not for the old pros among you, those who are on their second or third million words. By now they can make the keyboard sing with smooth and effective prose—or they have turned into hopeless hacks.

Rather, this is for the young, or for those of any age so new to writing that they sit transfixed before the keyboard. The words will not flow; they are extruded, one by one, and each must be bolted into place on a shaky structure. This is art? No, this is pain. This is despair. Panic is only one more ten-minute trance away.

I don't know if it will help or hurt to tell you that these stupors never really disappear. At any time in your writing life, even when words seem to dance at your command, you might suffer another seizure. By that time, though, you will have learned that the relapse is only temporary, that your prose will flow again—and you will not panic.

But how do you get there? How do you work out your writing muscles so that sentences and paragraphs appear almost effortlessly on the paper before you? The standard answer is, you learn to write by writing, just as you learn to skate by skating. You just put the skates on and shove off, and when you fall, you get up and start again.

The flaw in this analogy is that when you start to skate you can practice on your own, for your own sake. You need not wait until somebody asks you to skate to the store and get a dozen eggs. In writing, though, too many novices believe they cannot write unless they have some literary errand to run, some assignment. So when the assignment comes, they choke. They can't write because they haven't written, and they haven't written because they didn't have an assignment.

But, you protest, you had to write in school: paragraphs, essays, stories for the student paper. And, of course, you write now when an editor gives you a story to do. Believe me, if you write only when an editor tells you to write, you will never be a writer. (And when the editor sees how you stumble through the little stories you get to do, you will get fewer and fewer assignments.)

If you want to break out of this circle of futility, the obvious answer is that you must devise writing exercises that you can perform on your own, when

nobody is looking. You have to develop a fluency—
and a confidence that you are fluent.

Forty years ago, a writer named Jack Woodford
used to counsel young writers to start by writing a
novel, not necessarily to get it published, but for the
value of the exercise. A novel, Woodford advised, is
"the best possible way to learn to write without getting caught at it." By the time the beginner finishes
the last chapter, Woodford reasoned, he will realize
that the first chapter stinks.

> That will be because during the course of
> the writing of the thing, he will have
> picked up a lot of prose trickery, which he
> can then use to good purpose in rewriting
> the first chapter—and most of the rest . . .
> until, perhaps, happily enough, when he
> gets to the end of the second version he
> will recognize the same condition . . . and
> rewrite again.

The principle is sound, but unless your ambition is
to write a novel, this exercise might not be the best
way to limber up. You would have to worry about
character and plot, among other things, and these con-
straints might impede your effort to make words appear on paper easily. Remember, it's fluency you are
after now.

Keeping a journal is another way to practice writing. Put down everything you can remember that happened today. Or try to write an accurate account (or even a fanciful one) of some scene you witnessed: Set the scene, describe the characters, quote their dialog. Do this every day.

You might even try an exercise that occupied my time one whole summer between my freshman and sophomore years. My problem then was that the typewriter seemed to be a barrier between my brain and the paper. It intimidated me. (Actually, of course, it was the writing process that intimidated me; the typewriter was just the symbol.) I wanted to intimidate it, to turn it into a tool that would obey me instantly, an extension of my central nervous system. I wanted immediate transfer of thought to paper.

So I tried this: I would close the door to my room, put paper in the machine, and start to write *at once*. I did not ponder what to write; I just tried to record every thought that crossed my mind, no matter how personal. (I was careful to burn these works before they could fall into parental hands.) It was like daydreaming on paper, free-association writing: no structure, no topic, no inhibitions. Just write/think/write, day after day.

I found, of course, that I could never record *every* thought as my mind veered this way and that. Thoughts are too slippery. But with practice I got better at it, turning out page after page of gibberish until, by the end of summer, I thought I had achieved a certain freedom from fear and restraint. Sitting before the typewriter now seemed an opportunity to write rather than an invitation to terror.

But once liberated, the young writer reaches another perilous stage of development. He must now learn to discipline himself, paradoxical as that may sound. Otherwise, the young writer, giddy with his new power, may come to believe that any thought that flashes through his mind becomes pure gold once it is committed to paper. So he must rein in, as the late Henry Justin Smith put it many years ago in a piece that influenced me (and these observations) a great deal.

By self-discipline, I mean in the use of grammar (of course), precise word usage, sound sentence structure —all the things I talked about earlier. Now, though, I mean something more: learning to express each thought concisely, to drive each sentence home clearly and effectively, with no unnecessary words.

Some established writers suggest writing poetry, even simple doggerel, as a control exercise. You might try sonnets. Even limericks, which are not only fun but good training. Or get a book of Robert W. Service's ballads and try that format. ("Back of the bar, in a solo game, sat Dangerous Dan McGrew.") What would you write about? Anything—what the governor is up to, the stupidity of playing on artificial turf, the madness of Washington National Airport, your love life—anything that will force you to express your thoughts within a confined space, making each word count. You can throw it all away, of course, but you'll keep the language control these exercises will teach you.

The best control exercise I found as a young writer was headline writing—not just to learn to write headlines (although I did), but to practice expressing ideas clearly in a space dictated by the width of the column and the size of the type. That pressure will really put a writer to the test.

Example: One paper I worked for featured a column that ran on the left side of page one, right up by the nameplate. This was in the days of eight narrow columns, so the number of letters in the head was limited to begin with. A box around the head chipped away even more space.

One day the columnist turned in a Memorial Day piece about a long-abandoned cemetery he had found, which he described in detail, right down to the iris planted many years ago when the cemetery still received Memorial Day visitors. It was a good mood piece, but in that upper-left column it presented a real challenge to the headline writer, a skilled editor named Tom Kiene. Kiene met the challenge with a head that condensed the mood piece to its essence:

> Iris Nod
> In Silent
> Benison

Had the headline writer enjoyed the luxury of twice that many words, the chances are he could not have produced anything half as good as that.

That is the kind of control I was trying to learn in my private headline-writing exercises (another idea I got from something Henry Justin Smith wrote). I would clip scores of stories out of newspapers and discard their headlines. I added to this collection every day until I had a mass of headless stories from several newspapers—and I had forgotten what the original heads said.

Each evening (I worked days as a reporter) I would spend an hour or so on these stories, picking them out of the pile at random. I might decide that on one I'd write a ten-character, three-line head, and on the next I'd write to a 14 count, and so on. And I would write and rewrite headlines within a strict head count until I was satisfied that I had packed as much information as possible, clearly expressed, into that narrow space. Then I'd throw them away and start on a new batch the next night.

So try headlines, if writing poetry doesn't appeal to you as a training exercise. If you can learn to compress the meaning of a 500-word story into six or eight short words, you will have acquired a fine writing skill.

Those, then, are the two self-development efforts I think are essential. First, liberate yourself; break out of your word jam by forcing yourself to write thousands of words until the mere flicker of a thought automatically becomes real words on paper. Second, when you are liberated, when the words flow as if you had flipped a switch, learn to restrain yourself, to get control of that flow of words so they can be put to any task.

Struggling with these exercises (on your own time, of course, since you probably will have to earn a living) may not strike you as the most thrilling way to spend your evenings. This is tough work. But I assume you mean it when you say you want to be a writer.

INDEX

INDEX